Praise

"Finance may be one cf the oldest industries, but its ability to continually innovate is what keeps it at the forefront of the global economy. As technology and fintech disrupt traditional models, understanding these frontier innovations becomes crucial. Daniel's book is an essential resource for anyone looking to stay educated on the latest developments in the SPAC space. His deep analysis of the evolving landscape, especially under new regulatory challenges, makes this work invaluable for both veterans and newcomers alike. For those of us who have seen the industry evolve from the trading floor to the digital realm, this is a must-read."
— **Michael Wu**, Founder & CEO,
Amber Group

"Daniel has the perfect background in structuring and the SPAC scars to prove it—he is qualified to guide anyone through this minefield."
— **Jonathan Paul**, co-Founder and CEO,
Adatos.AI

THE DREAMS PROTOCOL

Daniel Mamadou-Blanco

How to
Secure Equity
Capital from
SPACs
and Qualified
Institutional
Investors

R^ethink

First published in Great Britain in 2024
by Rethink Press (www.rethinkpress.com)

For my family, my friends, and my business partners

Disclaimer

This book promotes the use of special purpose acquisition companies (SPACs) as a means for companies to become publicly listed on US exchanges such as Nasdaq. However, entering into a merger or acquisition agreement with a SPAC involves significant financial and legal considerations. It is essential that readers consult with a qualified corporate finance adviser before making any decisions related to SPAC transactions.

The references to publicly listed companies and their stocks within this book are intended solely for illustrative purposes and do not constitute a recommendation or endorsement to buy, sell, or trade in any securities mentioned. Readers should not rely on any statements or information presented herein to make investment decisions related to these shares. It is strongly advised that readers receive professional advice before making any investment choices or engaging in trading activities. The author and publisher shall not be held liable for any investment decisions made based on the content of this book or any outcomes resulting from reliance on the information presented. While the author has made every effort to ensure the information is reliable, no guarantees are made regarding its accuracy or completeness. Readers are encouraged to verify any details independently.

Contents

Foreword

The US public markets benefit from its breadth and depth, but the number of public companies and retail investors have been shrinking exponentially in recent decades. The biggest beneficiaries have been private equity firms and investment bankers who mystify IPOs, creating toll ways and gatekeepers in an ecosystem that should pride itself on transparent and equitable market access.

In a perfect world, SPACs offer democratized access to the capital markets for both companies seeking capital and the investors who possess it. Companies can articulate their own unfiltered stories while achieving capital access. Investors can express their support for companies in a self-determined manner without an asymmetry of information (whereby investment banks provide projections and allocations only to their top trading relationships).

SPACs aspire to improve the capital markets, and few share that vision as passionately as Daniel Mamadou. I have grown to admire his creativity and tenacity, both in innovating toward a better structure and asking the "why not" questions that challenge us to be better. Over the past few years, Daniel has been a constant champion for his partners with an enthusiasm that has persevered through both good and bad times. I am excited for you to better understand SPACs through his lens!

Managing Director, Cohen Capital Markets

Prologue

In the last week of June 2024, the SPAC (special purpose acquisition company) crowd gathered at the Westchester Country Club in Rye, an idyllic location fifteen minutes away from Greenwich, where many hedge funds are based, and almost an hour away from Wall Street in New York City, where the bankers ply their trade. Over two days, industry players examined numerous topics related to SPACs in detail.

New rules, same game

On 1 July 2024, new rules affecting SPACs imposed by the Securities and Exchange Commission (SEC) went live. These rules say that a SPAC initial public offering (IPO) is the same as a regular IPO. As such, the PSLRA (Private Securities Litigation Reform Act,[1] which provides a safe harbor for forward-looking statements under the Securities Act of 1933 and the Securities Exchange Act of 1934) is not available. Furthermore, additional disclosure is required regarding dilution due to private investment in public equity (PIPE) transactions, material financing terms, board determination of the fairness of a deal, and financial projections. This new regime is not expected to affect the SPAC participants in a significant way, given that the industry has, by and large, operated on this basis since the beginning of the consultation period with the SEC more than two years ago. Additional rules that affect reverse takeovers and private vehicles having to file registration statements are coming into play. The application of the excise tax on trust redemptions for domestic entities has also been confirmed (but does not apply in the case of liquidation). These new rules improve the overall quality of the ecosystem and will go a long way toward making the SPAC more robust.

PIPEs too are affected by the new SEC guidelines. These are vital because they are used to solve minimum cash conditions and excessive redemption—there is no relationship between the amount of capital raised in a SPAC IPO versus the capital available for the merged entity after the de-SPAC merger. In 2020, average SPAC redemption rates were 38%; average redemption rates climbed to 94% last year, according to SPAC Research (newsletter February 2022).[2] This is also the basis for my view that, overall, SPACs' returns are being underestimated because most investors going into de-SPAC MergedCos do not get their stock at the $10 share price. SPACs sponsors get their stock well below $10, and PIPE investors get significant discounts depending on the type of structure they agree to.

The current dynamics have transformed SPACs into credit products mainly for hedge funds, which comprise the bulk of the shareholders at IPO. PIPEs are there to manage the "cash at close" condition (the minimum cash condition) and control the redemption rate of the SPAC. Because PIPEs have a dilutive impact, the SEC, which is focused on strengthening disclosure requirements, has proposed guidelines that would potentially characterize PIPE providers as underwriters, with the associated liability risk; this has had a significant impact on PIPE providers, who reacted pre-emptively and adjusted their exposure accordingly. In 2021, the average PIPE financing was $316 million; by 2022, that average had dropped to $65 million (according to a note circulated by Skadden "De-SPAC transaction trends in 2023").[3]

The other major obstacle for the PIPE market has been the safe harbor rules not applying to financial projections (how do you entice an investor if you can't show them what the future could look like?). Whereas traditionally PIPEs were straight equity purchases at a fixed price, today they come in various forms, such as convertibles and other structured financing solutions. They remain essential to any de-SPAC merger deal, and the uncertainty associated with the SEC's guidance on underwriter status means that it may take longer to arrange PIPE financing going forward.

The bottom line is that longer de-SPAC merger timelines must be assumed: delays are now a feature of the de-SPAC merger process, not an exception. Counterintuitively, the new SEC rules will result in less information sharing, impacting target selection.

At the SPAC Conference 2024,[4] hosted by DealFlow Events in June 2024, several sessions focused on what it takes to get a successful de-SPAC merger deal done: no lofty valuations or fanciful revenue projections, proper due diligence, and avoiding material misrepresentations. A lot of the suggestions were logical components of any professionally executed deal. However, there were also mentions of softer aspects, such as the credibility of the management team. Someone spoke of the need for MergedCos to have a strong CFO who can stand behind the numbers presented to investors. Target selection was another point highlighted, with several presenters urging SPACs to avoid thinly capitalized companies on the verge of running out of cash. One commentator brought up a factor that is almost always ignored: the after-merger trading conditions of the stock, ie, getting volume on trading and ensuring that the stock liquidity is there.

Regarding the future of the SPAC market, the consensus is that the new rules imposed by the SEC make things more complex. The reality is that the SPAC product has always been targeted at emerging private growth companies that cannot command the focus and attention of private equity and venture capital investors. The new rules aim to level the playing field with IPOs and to deter abusive participants. Yet, simultaneously, they may scare away some of the financing parties while affecting the makeup of the targets chosen for de-SPAC mergers going forward.

Still, the future for SPACs is bright: in 2023, there were 197 liquidations, and the average redemption rate was 94%.[5] In practice, that means $35 billion of capital has been recycled and is sitting in funds waiting to be redeployed. The SPAC ecosystem will continue to evolve and standards will improve. The new regime will increase SPAC IPO issuance, although we may not return to the crazy number of SPAC IPOs we saw in 2021. This regime also almost guarantees that new SPAC IPOs will be issued by companies incorporated in the Cayman Islands; the application of the excise tax to US domestic vehicles means that the Delaware SPAC is pretty much dead.

In 2021 we had 613 SPAC IPOs out of 968 total IPOs (63% of the total market). This was an outlier. By mid-year 2024, we have seen forty-six SPAC IPOs that have raised $6 billion in aggregate.[6] Yet, the market is still feeling the effects of that bumper year in 2021. As of June 2024, 102 SPACs with $8 billion locked in trust accounts were still searching for a deal. About 80% of these were scheduled to expire before December 2024.[7] This means that for private company founders and owners looking to go public, the opportunity has never been greater. Read on to find out how to maximize your chances of a successful merger with a SPAC.

Introduction

If you want to learn how to get in front of qualified institutional investors who have a mandate to invest millions in equity capital as minority shareholders in your company, and how to close the entire process in a record time, this book is for you.

You might be the founder or owner of a private company that requires significant capital to grow. You could be a majority shareholder, a CEO, a CFO, or a senior executive tasked with finding the best way to raise finance for the company. Essentially, you are the person who has the mandate and the agreement of the shareholders to explore all possible avenues to raise capital for the company to propel its growth. That company may be a startup, or it could have been operating for some time. Ideally, it is private.

What matters is that your company is in expansion mode and requires a significant equity capital boost.

I have worked as a capital markets officer and advised corporations for more than twenty years, covering Europe and Asia, including the Southeast Asian markets, Greater China, and Korea. I initially began my career in London before moving to Singapore and Hong Kong. I worked for over twenty years as a managing director in capital markets for several bulge-bracket banks, including Deutsche Bank, Goldman Sachs, Nomura Holdings, and Bank of Tokyo-Mitsubishi. Throughout my investment banking career, I have raised more than $30 billion in the form of equity capital, syndicated loans, bonds, and other financial instruments within the capital structure stack of companies. As a managing director focused on finding financing solutions for large corporations, I have assisted numerous companies in establishing the right foundations to ensure their capital access is flexible and plentiful.

During my time at Noble Group—in 2010, the largest trader of carbon steel material globally—I set up the Technology Materials division, where I spent ten years building up supply chains for industrial metals and minerals like lithium and cobalt, across South America, Australia, Africa, and Europe.

Raising capital can be a smooth process and does not have to be burdensome. Still, there is a common methodology that needs to be applied within any business. In my career, I have found that many private companies are unaware of this process. Beyond simply asking for bank loans, they are unprepared to face institutional investors from whom they can raise significant capital in the form of equity. Yet you, as the owner (or manager) of a private company that requires access to a substantial amount of capital, can correctly position your company to raise that capital. You can aspire to efficiently access millions of dollars in equity capital, thereby setting yourself up to never again have to struggle to raise the funds that your business needs.

My DREAMS protocol is a tried-and-tested approach to attracting institutional capital for private companies. It is focused on reaching out to a specific pool of investors: the institutional investors that have traditionally been the primary source of equity funding for the general economy. These are the ones that deploy capital in large ticket sizes. To get on their radar, you must have the right team onboard, the proper guidance, and the right approach. The DREAMS protocol is the right approach.

DREAMS stands for:

- **D:** Dataset, detail, documentation, and digital vault

- **R:** Risk, research, and reach out

- **E:** Evaluate and engage
- **A:** Align, advance, and agree
- **M:** Mobilize, materialize, and merge
- **S:** Seek sustainability

To give you a brief outline before we get into the details later in the book, the initial step consists of gathering all the relevant information and collating it into a data room. This houses all the documents that are key to evaluating a deal from the perspective of institutional investors. This step will take you through preparing the minimum viable information required to present the company and its business to potential strategic and institutional investors. The second step involves identifying the key risks of your business and researching critical market data, including the amount of capital available and the decision-makers controlling that capital. It also means analyzing the current market situation concerning investors' sentiment and their current appetite for equity risk to identify the institutional investors primed to invest in your company.

We then move on to the third phase, where you work on closely aligning your pitch to the requirements of the institutional investors who have signaled interest in your company. Once the relevant matches have been confirmed, it is time to connect with them. After engaging, we move to the next step, which involves agreeing on the deal, determining the details of the investment terms, and forming a broader arrangement regarding the company going forward. Once the agreement is signed, it is time to mobilize resources and materialize the transaction through careful and disciplined execution, leading to a merger. Finally, society, governments, and investors consider sustainability a key factor. Capital follows enterprises that sustainably generate profits and contribute to advancing society and reducing inequalities. Already, most publicly listed companies are compelled to explain their plans regarding sustainability. It is only a matter of time before this becomes an obligation for even private businesses.

The DREAMS protocol is a roadmap designed to get your company in the best possible position to access the capital you require by identifying the ideal institutional investors for your funding round. The process will also ensure you find the right time window to tap in terms of capital and locate the best partners to work with; you will choose the right location to get listed, and you will be able to make an informed decision about which service providers you contract. In addition, you will gain clarity concerning the costs associated with taking your company public and accessing institutional capital. This book also gives a realistic assessment of the availability of capital and level of investor interest for your business in terms of who can invest, how much they might be willing to invest, and at what valuation they will invest.

Even if you do not end up taking your company public, the benefits of implementing the tips and advice in this book will put you and your company in a much stronger position when it comes to communicating with shareholders, financiers, and capital providers going forward. These could be banks, lending agencies, state-owned and bilateral agencies, venture capital firms, investment funds, or family offices.

It's a win-win scenario. So let's get started.

PART ONE
DISRUPTIVE IDEAS

Professional investors are the key to SPACs, which in turn are the key to your company's future.

ONE

Why SPACs?

Imagine a small-town watchmaker who makes high-end luxury timepieces. Each watch has been carefully manufactured with noble materials and ultimate craftsmanship. It takes him time and effort to create a single watch but he also has to start selling the goods, generating income, and growing the business. He hires a salesperson who goes to the local farmers' market, where people buy fresh produce and affordable handmade crafts.

Guess what? He sells almost nothing. This is because he is fishing in the wrong pond. Instead, he should focus on attending luxury trade shows or visiting high-end shopping districts of the capital city, where affluent people who appreciate luxury items are more likely to be clients.

Finding the right pond

SPACs are the ultimate expression of an institutional investor willing and ready to deploy capital within a specific timeline. SPACs represent the right pond for entrepreneurs and companies seeking capital. Appendix 1 provides some background on the nature and history of SPACs, but let's begin by looking at them in a bit more detail.

Time and again, I come across founders, CEOs, and businesspeople who have been on the money-raising journey for the past year or two, going from one family office discussion to another, approaching private equity firms and a long list of "potential investors." The issue they face is that none of these investors has any urgent need to deploy their hard-earned capital. These entrepreneurs are fishing in the wrong pond. They should concentrate their efforts where the probability of success is mathematically high rather than wasting time on less fruitful prospects.

Don't spend your time talking to investors for whom there is no urgency to do a deal. Don't pitch to them repeatedly, go through various calls and video conferences, or an endless process where progress is slow and the tasks never-ending. These might be the right investors, but have you considered if it is the right *time* to approach them? These investors may have capital, but often they don't have the urgency to invest.

SPACs are different.

SPACs are your optimum choice because they have a deadline, plus they are ensconced within an ecosystem of institutional investors. Besides being institutional investors, SPACs typically bring private equity investors into the transaction once the target has been defined and when the merger discussion starts. By marketing your deal to a SPAC, you are also getting exposure: putting your business in front of the right audience of private equity investors. SPAC investors (the investors in the trust IPO) are also often subsidiaries of hedge funds. To complete that ecosystem, service providers, such as accountants and lawyers, can all refer your investment opportunity to other institutional investors. Even if you don't end up merging with a SPAC once you start the discussion to raise capital with them, you will reach the right audience of institutional investors who are ready to make investments. Any private equity firm brought into a deal data room by a SPAC sponsor is, by definition, looking to deploy capital.

This is completely different from going out in the wild and contacting family offices, for example, who have no specific timeline within which they need to close a deal. The same is true for many other types of investors. By going to SPACs first, you are entering through the front door of an ecosystem of institutional investors simultaneously looking to deploy capital and looking for an exit. SPACs are like beacons that attract a wider pool of professional and sophisticated investors to consider interesting transactions together; they exchange views and opinions and refer investment opportunities to one another. That is why it makes sense to knock on the door of the SPAC market first when you're looking to raise money. There, you'll get the relevant exposure to the various private equity firms that navigate around the SPACs to provide PIPE to the different transactions that come to the table. PIPE investors are always interested in understanding their exit strategy. The standard exit strategies for private investment are either a trade sale or a public listing. For this reason, private equity firms are constantly in discussions with SPAC sponsors. Some groups manage both ends of the aisle by having both a private equity team and a SPAC team whose function is to take over parts of the portfolio companies that sit on the private equity side of the business.

The evolution of SPACs

SPACs are not get-rich-quick schemes. The term SPAC does have some negative connotations, due to the historical link to "blank-check" companies with no investor protections. This background is explained in more detail in Appendix 1, but essentially, the often-unscrupulous securities firms that promoted these transactions could be loose with their quality standards and aggressively promoted questionable companies to unsophisticated investors, overstating their valuations and making false promises. This type of securities firm was usually called a "boiler room."

New investor safeguards

After significant investor losses, the SEC stepped in to rein in these practices Over the years, financiers have worked together with the SEC to strengthen the rail guards around blank-check companies, and SPACs evolved to provide increased transparency and more safeguards for investors. These efforts have also established minimum quality standards for the private companies that become publicly listed through merging with a listed SPAC. This process is also called a "de-SPAC merger."

Back in the day, SPACs were able to make all sorts of forward-looking statements in their marketing presentations to investors. Over time, the SEC has focused on making sure that SPACs are subject to the same level of disclosure as standard IPOs; as a result, today there is almost no regulatory arbitrage between a SPAC and a regular IPO. The attributes that make SPACs more attractive than standard IPOs are the speed of execution and the certainty in the valuation of the deal.

As of the 2024 regulation, the alignment of interest between the SPAC sponsors, the investors in the SPAC, and the shareholders of the private company has become completely transparent. Under this regime, SPACs aren't the get-rich-quick schemes the financial press sometimes likes to refer to; instead, they have become an alternative way to attract funding from qualified institutional investors for private companies that are growing at an accelerated pace.

Redemption rights

The redemption right is crucial to the alignment of interest between parties; it enables the shareholders in the SPAC to decide whether they like the transaction once it is presented to them and whether they want to finance its acquisition. When a SPAC raises capital via an IPO, the participants in the SPAC have no visibility in the target business at the time of investing in the trust; they simply don't know which company will eventually be merged into that listed vehicle.

In the past, investors did not have this redemption right and relied on the SPAC sponsors' track record. Today, their right to redeem allows them to decide whether to finance the company going forward (once they have reviewed the target); they also have the right to determine if they will back the merger.

SPAC shareholders typically get an incentive for having locked up their capital and provided financial backup for the vehicle during the time it has taken the SPAC sponsors to identify the right target to merge with. From their perspective, SPAC sponsors ("financiers") get to negotiate the valuation but also have a vested interest in ensuring that the post-merger performance of the publicly listed stock is good.

All SPACs are priced at $10 per share at the time of issue, irrespective of the deal valuation. Both investors in the SPAC and shareholders of the privately held company share the same interest in seeing the share price go above $10 once the merger has been approved because they collectively receive distributed primary shares in the newly formed merged entity (often called MergedCo).

The sponsors of the SPACs also get rewarded with primary shares of MergedCo, which are often locked up for a lengthy period. The lockup provisions are usually extended to other participants in the deal, including the owners of the private company that is seeking the merger. Essentially, everyone is locked up, and no individual shareholder can sell their shares in the market immediately after the merger has been approved. That means no one is getting rich quickly.

Essentially, SPACs have evolved in important ways and today, they are regulated instruments supervised by the SEC in the United States. It is fair to say that in the past, SPACs were associated with questionable practices from dodgy securities firms. Today, the authorities have caught up and closed the regulatory arbitrage gap between SPACs and IPOs, making SPACs a recognized mechanism for private companies to go public.

What do SPACs want?

The information they want isn't necessarily what you'd expect. Often, the primary focus of prospective clients approaching me is capital raising. They typically have a deck that would have been prepared internally, or sometimes externally by a corporate finance boutique or a specialist advisory firm. The deck contains all sorts of information, including the market needs addressed by the company, information about the company's operations, financial projections, and so on. Sometimes, a data room containing extensive confidential documents is also available. Finally, there is a teaser. Having all this information in a form that can be safely shared with external parties is a standard part of the capital-raising process.

A deck like this does not usually cover the top concerns of typical SPAC institutional investors, as they have different priorities when it comes to deploying capital. While interested in the business details, they assess opportunities differently. SPAC institutional investors have a methodology by which they decide whether to pursue an opportunity, and they spend time and money on doing due diligence for a particular merger opportunity.

It is critical for you, as the private business owner seeking to raise capital from SPAC sponsors, to understand what these priorities are. You must provide sponsors with the information they need to move to the next stage of their decision-making process. This essential information will determine whether your company presents a valid opportunity to go public through a merger with their vehicle, unlocking the capital you require in the process.

The biggest focus for SPAC institutional investors is whether the company with which they intend to merge—your company—can be successfully certified under the Public Company Accounting Oversight Board (PCAOB) of the US. This is the US standard used by the SEC as a condition for approving a company to go public on one of the US exchanges. The implication of this is that you need to have audited financials, ideally under one of the standards that are easy to assess using the US accounting standards. The PCAOB audit is the gateway to a transaction with a SPAC where you merge your private business and become listed on a US stock exchange.

SPAC sponsors focus on this point because the translation of local financial statements to a US accounting standard (and the subsequent PCAOB audit) can be a lengthy process, which massively impacts the timeline of the transaction. As mentioned, SPACs are subject to time limits, so understanding how long the PCAOB audit will take is crucial for SPAC sponsors. If they assess that it will take too long, they may pass on the deal, irrespective of how attractive the company's business is. One big reason why audits can be complex is the number of subsidiaries a business handles;

the more complicated the corporate structure, especially if it involves foreign subsidiaries, the more difficult it is to perform the PCAOB audit.

Another factor to consider is the availability of qualified auditors to do the job. In the past few years, auditing firms have been heavily solicited and, in general, they have more than enough work and requests for new assignments; as a result, they can be pretty selective when deciding whether or not to take on a mandate.

I cannot stress enough how important this aspect of the decision-making process is for SPAC sponsors. Irrespective of how attractive your business proposition or your product is, or even how good your numbers and financials are, none of it will matter if a certified PCAOB auditor cannot review and approve your books. Remember, the SPAC sponsor and the board of directors of the publicly listed company are responsible for providing financials and an accurate and transparent picture of the financial situation of the merged entity. They commonly and severally share civil responsibility and liability for doing so. This is why it is vital to tackle this aspect of the transaction upfront before moving on to other details, such as the valuation.

A second and equally important point regarding the information package is the data room, specifically the financial model and projections. Giving forward-looking forecasts to the market has been one of the most controversial aspects differentiating SPACs from traditional IPOs. In 2020 and 2021, many companies that had gone public using SPAC mergers failed to achieve the revenue numbers advertised in their financial projections. The projections bore no resemblance to what happened in real life once the company had gone public. In many cases, none of the customer orders that had been touted by the businesses before the merger ever materialized, even partially. While there were good reasons why some companies missed their estimated earnings, in many cases, the reason was simply that the projections shown to prospective investors during the merger process were fanciful, wishful thinking rather than anchored in reality. This led to a spate of class action lawsuits, where investors alleged that they had been misled. One example is the case of Waitr's acquisition by Lancadia Holdings Inc, where the board of the SPAC was accused of making statements that were over optimistic and misleading regarding the company's health and business prospects.[8]

It is no longer possible for SPACs to advertise forward-looking statements such as financial projections. However, that does not remove the fact that the SPAC sponsors will want to understand how quickly your business is expected to grow and how risky it is. They will also form a view on how qualifiable it is by the SEC and will use the financial model and its assumptions to get an idea of this.

The financial model needs to be built in such a way that the inputs and assumptions to calculate best, worst, and middle scenarios cases can be easily changed. I recommend that your financial model be constructed so that assumptions can be changed dynamically: variable inputs concerning price curves, product costs, exchange rates, and market rates can be adjusted according to the different scenarios explored, and business simulations can be run.

The data room will also contain all other important information related to the business and its operations. In older and more complicated business operations, there could be hundreds, if not thousands, of documents and contracts. One of the most critical tasks will be bringing forward the contracts that best represent the company's status.

Having a list of key contracts that back up the revenues and the forward-looking pipeline is vital. Long-term offtake contracts give the business a solid revenue source to back up projections made in the financial model, while long-term purchase contracts help present an image of stability and sustainability for the company going forward.

What does the business currently look like, in terms of existing contracts? Organizing the data room to clearly indicate customers' purchase orders is a good start. You must specify where the Memoranda of Understanding and the Letters of Intent are stored.

The quality of the counterparties to these contracts is essential, as the strength of these agreements can help validate and sustain the valuation of pre-revenue upcoming business. You also need to identify any restrictions imposed on your business.

If the business is a patent-heavy or tech-heavy type of company, the patents will be another business-related factor. What are the unique selling propositions for the company's line of products? It is essential to store all relevant information so that you can validate the present and future cash flows and the company's pipeline.

During the due diligence period, your VP of sales or business development head may be asked to have a conversation with the SPAC sponsor. In some cases, they may also want to externally validate the existence of a business relationship between your company and its customers. In areas or fields involving highly confidential information or trade secrets, it is vital to ensure the relevant mechanisms are in place to avoid leaking or losing information. A detailed assessment of the risks that affect the business is also crucial. Finally, the sustainability of the operations under different circumstances must be considered.

Currency = faster growth

By going public, you place your business in the position of being able to grow faster through acquisitions because going public means that you create trade-able securities that can be used as a form of currency to pay for services, goods, and, more importantly, acquisitions.

Using your publicly listed stock to acquire other companies and businesses gives you a serious advantage over your competitors. Issuing more shares is much easier for listed companies than most private companies. Business owners often ignore this point as their focus is on growing the business organically. They usually underestimate the value of using this form of currency for acquisitions, or to settle obligations. There will be times when the sector in which you operate becomes the darling of investors and speculators, granting your company a higher valuation than it deserves. This can be a good moment to consider making acquisitions partly or wholly funded by shares. This ability to use your shares as currency with an objective valuation to make acquisitions is a factor that cannot be overlooked in managing your business and pursuing company growth.

A final point to consider is that once public, the time required for you to execute another capital raise is significantly reduced. Of course, many factors related to the company will come into play. Still, you can quickly raise additional capital by making private placements to sophisticated investors without seeking shareholders' approval, provided you operate within the limits of the rules applied by the exchange. Nasdaq's "20%

rule" means that offerings below that threshold are not necessarily subject to shareholders' approval.[9]

Public companies attract institutional investors

Private companies in expansion mode face a series of challenges regarding the financial side of things: they have to balance growth with profitability, while at the same time carefully managing cash flow. Often, they find themselves spending money at a faster rate than the speed of their revenues, which creates a liquidity issue unless they have straightforward and ready access to capital on terms and conditions that are sustainable. In addition, due to their private nature, they are perceived to be less transparent than their publicly listed peers. The perception from lenders and investors is that the standards of corporate governance and internal risk controls may not be as high as they would be if the company were trading on a stock exchange.

Valuation can also be an issue when raising equity capital. Often, private companies raise capital in various rounds from a few shareholders each time, which means that many investors do not verify the valuation used. Typically, the valuation results from a direct agreement between the company and the group of investors coming into the particular financing round. This opaque process often leads to discrepancies between the public market value of the company and the figure at which the latest funding round has been conducted. A great example is WeWork, which reached an enormously high valuation of $47 billion as a private company before getting a reality check when it went public at a valuation of $9 billion. Private markets had massively overvalued the company, and the public markets corrected it.

The initial investors in a private company are usually unable to conduct thorough due diligence due to the developing nature of the business. The longer the company stays private, the higher the risk of becoming overvalued over time. Another factor contributing to those discrepancies is hype, which, when combined with a lack of availability of the stock and optimistic projections, can create a distorted picture of the company. These discrepancies occur when raising capital as a private company, and when the number of investors involved is small; these investors can be less informed, which creates the potential for overvaluation.

When that private company then needs to access a large amount of capital in one go, it suddenly faces a situation whereby it has to address the needs of a different type of investor. It must face a large number of potential financiers as opposed to having one-on-one conversations and bilateral discussions with anchor investors. They're dealing here with institutional investors. These investors will scrutinize the company's business model in a specific way. They have a completely different approach to early angels and venture capital (VC) investors. Their analysts will review the company's projections in great detail, challenge the assumptions used to draft these financial projections, scrutinize the company's books, and revalidate the significant contracts and customer orders. They will ultimately mark-to-market the company to its competition and sector by evaluating and comparing the management and financial ratios against comparable publicly listed companies.

Publicly listed companies benefit from the fact that this work is usually done by external research analysts, which helps to provide an objective view of the business. A private company doesn't have the same advantages as a publicly listed company when tapping equity markets that are in "risk-on mode" and where investor appetite is high, even if capital is abundant.

Accessing funds as a publicly listed company is a more straightforward process: you pick up the phone and call your capital markets banker; they send you an engagement letter detailing their fees, and you agree on a discount to the market valuation of the company for a capital raise. Once all is decided, they will market the deal and take you on a roadshow—physical, virtual, or hybrid—*et voilà*! You can raise tens of millions in capital this way when you are a publicly listed company. In contrast, a private company requires a full review, making it generally more expensive.

TWO
SPACs And IPOs

In the future, I predict that every business will be virtually public and that SPACs and IPOs will be essentially the same thing.

As society and the world move toward complete transparency, the information of most companies will be accessible simply because consumers want and need more transparency regarding businesses and the practices that surround them. Today, large private corporations provide operational updates with the same frequency as publicly listed companies. Access to capital is the primary driver that fuels a business and allows it to grow. Banks, institutional investors, and other capital providers are now ensuring that capital is laid out for general ventures that are good for society.

Think of the United Nations' Sustainable Development Goals (SDGs). They provide a blueprint for society to achieve prosperity and emphasize the collaboration between businesses, civil society, and governments. They also provide a framework for monitoring the progress toward sustainable development. Today, many banks look at SDGs attached to a company's mission statement as part of their evaluation before granting a loan. The cost of money is also increasingly tied to the social aspects of the business; a good example is green bond finance, whereby lenders provide cheaper capital when borrowers agree to dedicate the proceeds to funding operations that are more efficient from an emissions perspective. This approach requires careful monitoring of the carbon footprint of the company's operations, which in turn means more transparency.

The implications for all businesses, including private ones, are clear: be transparent and be compliant. As a business owner, you must do this if you want to grow, so you might as well become a publicly listed business and take advantage of the benefits this offers. The logical conclusion is that you should merge your company with a publicly listed vehicle because, in the future, you will have similar reporting requirements, even if you remain private.

Choosing between a SPAC or IPO

Going public means either launching an IPO or merging with a SPAC, an already listed company. In terms of which path you decide to follow, the choice is yours, but there are several factors to consider. When we analyze the differences between a SPAC and an IPO, five exciting points come to the surface:

Difference 1: The type of shares in a de-SPAC vs an IPO

The de-SPAC merger is the act of merging a private company with a publicly listed SPAC. In a de-SPAC merger deal, the main event is the SPAC entity's acquisition of your privately held business. This results in a merger where primary shares of the merged entity are distributed to shareholders. The capital that funds the merger would have been raised from institutional investors sometime before the event and kept in a trust vehicle. This capital is unlocked once the merger has been agreed upon and the deal has been submitted to a vote by the shareholders of the listed SPAC.

An IPO, on the other hand, is a single capital-raising event. In that event, the private company's new shares (again called primary shares) are offered for sale to the public. Secondary shares are also sold, allowing early investors to exit the business. The main practical implication is that not all of the proceeds of the IPO get to be reinvested in the business. This is an essential consideration for you as a company owner.

Difference 2: Timing

Another significant difference between SPACs and IPOs is that SPACs are bound by time: they must complete a merger within a stipulated timeline, typically limited to thirty-six months. If this doesn't happen, the SPAC investors can redeem their original investment at the end of that period. This means that both SPAC sponsors and shareholders are motivated to do a deal and so act differently from other investors who may not have any urgent need to deploy their capital. The stakeholders in a SPAC sit under a ticking clock and have limited time to identify a private business suitable for taking public, negotiate agreeable terms with all parties, and execute a merger deal between their entity and the target. For any business owner looking to merge with a SPAC, it is prudent to figure out the expiration date of the SPAC vehicle before going too deep into the conversation concerning a potential merger.

Market conditions drive the timing of IPOs. As a business owner, when you consider raising capital with an IPO, you must wait for the right window to go public. Because that window opens and shuts quickly, depending on market conditions, it is difficult to establish a "going public" date with certainty. In general, with IPOs, the process can last between a few weeks and a few months, due to the uncertainty presented by market conditions.

Difference 3: Marketing process

From a marketing point of view, the main advantage of SPACs is that you don't have to do a marketing roadshow. As shareholders vote on the merger deal once the target has been identified, there is little need for upfront marketing. The shareholders rely on the judgment of the SPAC sponsors to choose the right target, and they have redemption rights anyway. In an IPO, the underwriters and the investment bankers bringing the company to the market need to test the waters; they also need to market the project to their investors and gauge the level of interest. Thus, they have to conduct extensive (and expensive) global roadshows, which can be time consuming.

The clearest evidence of the superior qualities of SPACs versus IPOs concerning marketing process is that during the COVID-19 pandemic years (2020–22), there were more SPAC deals done than in the entire history of SPACs since public markets have existed in the US. Faced with the impossibility of traveling and conducting roadshows, companies and investment bankers relied on the unique qualities of SPACs to raise the badly needed capital to keep their businesses running.

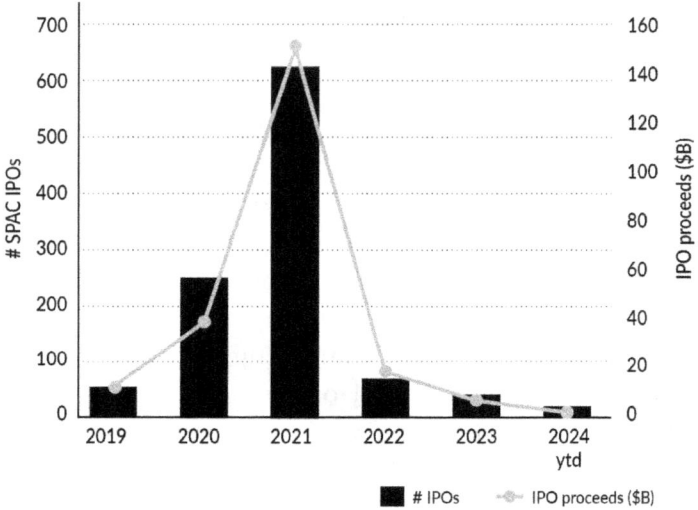

Number of SPAC IPOs
Graph by Daniel Mamadou-Blanco, data source: SEC

Difference 4: Regulatory regime

The next area of distinction between SPACs and traditional IPOs is their respective regulations. SPACs historically have fewer reporting obligations than IPOs, though the SEC has recently updated the rules to bring SPACs' reporting requirements to the same level as IPOs'. Previously, SPACs could advertise future revenue projections and make forward-looking statements, whereas IPOs could not. The latest regulatory changes now make it difficult, if not impossible, for SPACs to do this. Overall, as of 2024, SPACs are on essentially the same level as IPOs in terms of compliance.

Difference 5: Costs

The final point of differentiation between SPACs and traditional IPOs is the cost. The costs of launching and merging a private business with a SPAC are usually known upfront, whereas the costs of an IPO depend on the timeline required to finalize the process. Early on, the private company owner needs to establish both visibility and a clear understanding of the costs of the de-SPAC merger. Although most of the de-SPAC merger costs will be covered by the proceeds resulting from the capital raised at the time of the merger, it is essential not to let these spiral out of control.

This last point also highlights the importance of two critical aspects of the merger agreement: the "net cash at close" and the "closing expenses." We will look at these topics in more detail later in the book, but there is a need for a net amount of cash at the close that covers the closing expenses and the working capital requirement for the business to function going forward.

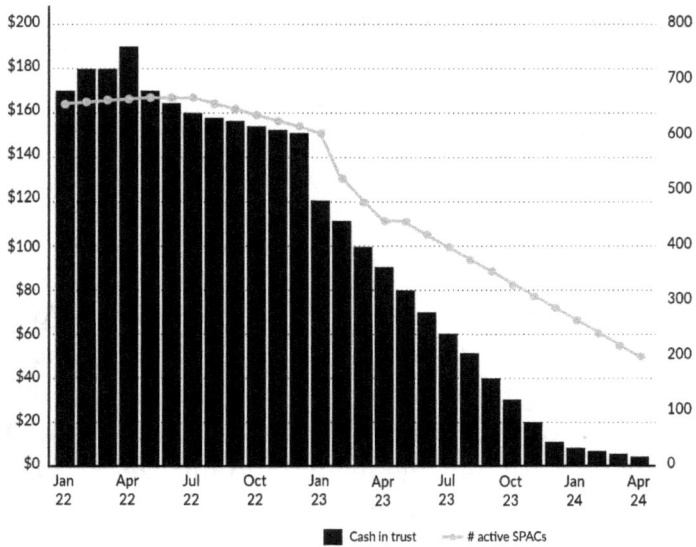

Value of active SPACs and cash in trust
Graph by Daniel Mamadou-Blanco, data source: SEC

I expect that SPACs and IPOs will continue to con-
verge in terms of regulations, but they will remain
distinct avenues for private businesses to go public;
the two main drivers in the decision to use a SPAC
instead of an IPO will be the size of the transaction
and the speed of execution required by the sponsors.
For small to medium-sized businesses, the SPAC avenue presents more advantages than the IPO, given the
reduced costs, the certainty and speed of execution,
and the likely lower capital requirements.

Speed and cost

Due to the flexibility in the execution process, it is possible to go public via a SPAC within a few months. However, this depends on the current status of the private business. If your company has its books in order, if you've recently conducted an audit, and assuming that you are using a globally recognized accounting standard (such as IFRS), then it is reasonably straightforward to have your accounts reviewed independently under the PCAOB audit standard.

The PCAOB audit process is one of the main gating points for any de-SPAC merger process and also represents one of the major cost components. Typically, auditors will take a fixed fee and seldom a performance fee. In practical terms, this means that they need to be paid at the time of the audit, ie, before the merger, and their costs are rarely deductible from the final proceeds.

Other costs attached to the de-SPAC merger include fees and retainers for investment bankers, accountants, bookkeepers, and lawyers. These costs can quickly spiral out of control, so it is crucial to request budget estimates from each service provider and agree on fee caps whenever possible.

Generally, you can defer the bulk of the costs to the merger date and pay these fees out of the proceeds of the cash obtained from the trust post-redemption by the shareholders of the SPAC. Some vendors will also agree that part of their costs can be compensated in the form of shares in the merged company instead of cash.

Contrary to popular opinion, going public with a SPAC is not costly. Of course, you need to keep costs under control, as you do in any business situation, and this book offers relevant guidance to help you avoid paying unnecessary fees.

Go west for the capital

SPACs are a relatively old financial concept with a controversial reputation, which sometimes has not been a benefit. As we learned earlier, the original form of SPACs was what is called a "blank-check company." First emerging in the '80s, these companies were used to bring private businesses to public markets quickly. SPACs feature in a lot of literature and movies that portray shady operations where dubious securities brokers sell illiquid business to naïve retail investors (see Appendix 1).

Over time, the SEC has worked with industry representatives and some financial sponsors to improve the regulation around SPACs and make them more transparent, with fairer terms for stakeholders and, more importantly, to bring additional protections for investors. Today, in a SPAC structure, the cash raised must stay contained in a trust, which is not accessible to the management of the SPAC. When the SPAC team has identified a private company to merge with, the SPAC investors and shareholders have the right to review the proposed business and can vote either in favor or against the transaction. They also have the option to take their money back, with interest (the "redemption right"). As a result, investors' interests are better protected.

Looking at the regulatory regimes of SPACs for other major markets, including the United Kingdom, the Netherlands, Hong Kong, and Singapore, the applicable rules sometimes make it more challenging to execute a de-SPAC merger than going public via a traditional IPO process. Although many other jurisdictions have recently introduced SPAC legislation, none can measure up to the US regarding regulation, depth of the capital markets, the number and variety of listing venues, and the number of institutional investors. For this reason, the US is currently the best jurisdiction in the world in which to execute a de-SPAC merger, so "go west" and de-SPAC on a US exchange.

In 2021, the number of SPACs issued boomed, and the volume of capital raised through SPACs in that one year alone was 613, more than the sum of all SPACs issued in the previous fifteen years in the US.[10] The pandemic seemed to have the impact of boosting the popularity of SPACs as a way to take companies public, and regulators worldwide began to imitate the SEC, implementing their own versions of SPACs adapted to local rules. Exchanges in Singapore, Hong Kong, Amsterdam, Milan, Madrid, and Paris followed the trend and developed local SPAC regulations. Yet the SPAC IPO boom didn't really happen outside of the US, and volumes of SPAC deals remained low, according to official data from the respective stock exchanges in France, the UK, Hong Kong, and the Netherlands.[11,12] It seems that regulators failed to see the advantages of enabling specific SPAC regulations that could compete with the established IPO regime and prove a more accessible (read "less safe") way for companies to issue shares to the public.

The US regulatory regime is ahead of the rest of the world regarding SPACs, and it will remain the leader for years to come simply because it has a longer tradition of balancing financial innovation and safety. The US SPAC regime is more flexible than its counterparts elsewhere, putting SPACs on a similar (but not equivalent) level to IPOs, providing a comparable level of protection to investors. This makes it a unique and attractive product for private companies that want to go public in the US in a relatively short timeframe.

The DREAMS protocol helps you grow

The discipline and the work needed to bring a private company up to the standards of a publicly listed company results in a win-win for all shareholders and stakeholders. In following the DREAMS protocol (which we will explore in depth in Chapter 5) to raise equity capital, the company and its owners go through an introspection process, where every aspect of operations is scrutinized from the perspective of a long-term institutional investor. In addition, you follow the rigorous steps to ensure that your company is fit to become a publicly listed company. The reasons why a merger with a SPAC may fail vary, but failure can often be attributed to the SPAC sponsors themselves and not necessarily to the private company that seeks the public listing. For example, a failure to merge could be related to insufficient capital being raised when the transaction closes. Another common reason is a disagreement over the merger valuation. Similarly, a dispute between the parties regarding the path forward for the company once the merger has occurred could be another deal stopper.

But a failure to reach a deal and merge on your first attempt does not mean the end of the process. After a period of self-examination, filling any obvious holes, and fixing glaring issues, you can revisit the transaction. In fact, you will be better positioned to execute the deal the second time around because once you have reached that point, you should have fully audited your books and remedied specific issues related to the company's corporate governance; you may have already passed a PCAOB audit; and you most certainly will have built a data room and spoken with potential long-term institutional investors. You will have received and acted upon candid feedback about your business. Essentially, you have come out of your shell and put your company out there in the open for the world to see. All these actions should contribute to removing the obstacles that could prevent your company from becoming successfully listed, putting you ahead of the pack for next time.

Attempting to fund your business growth by following the DREAMS protocol benefits you as a company as it forces you to diagnose the current status. The discipline required to go through the process and the transparency it injects are improvements in corporate governance, which will have a positive impact for years.

De-SPAC for already listed companies

A major misconception regarding SPACs and IPOs is that a company that is already listed cannot do a primary listing anywhere else and must instead establish a dual listing, which would bring no notable improvement in the valuation of its market capitalization (and share price). Nothing could be further from the truth. While for companies that are already exchange-listed, it makes sense to focus on dual listing to expand their shareholder base, there are several examples of entities that are already public and list a specific portion of the business in a different market, on a different exchange, to unlock the value of those assets.

A discrepancy between valuations is a direct function of investor preferences in particular exchanges. For example, real estate-related assets tend to be better valued on the Singapore Exchange than on the Tokyo Stock Exchange, regardless of the actual location of the underlying assets. This is because, over the years, the Singapore Exchange has specialized in listings related to real estate. In the process, it has attracted the attention of global investors and, as a result, international real estate companies. Another example is the Nasdaq, which has become the preferred venue for high-growth companies. Essentially, the gap in valuations between exchanges can be a helpful driver of the decision of whether to go public via a SPAC or pursue a dual listing for companies already trading on an exchange.

As the managing director of a publicly listed company, you can use the de-SPAC merger process to raise additional capital by getting listed on an exchange, like the Nasdaq or the New York Stock Exchange, in addition to your home listing. Of course, there needs to be an economically valid reason to undertake such an exercise: better multiples or a higher market capitalization are typical motivators. Access to additional funding is also why smaller companies operating in highly speculative and volatile environments choose to merge with Nasdaq-listed SPACs. Entering into such a transaction brings further benefits; for example, it allows you to reach out to new investors located away from your home market, who would otherwise be unable to invest in your company. Many of the companies that engage in the exploration of minerals and metals and that are listed on the Toronto Stock Exchange, the London Junior AIM (alternative investment market), or the Australian Stock Exchange tend to remain out of reach for US-based investors, mainly due to regulations that prevent the unrestricted sale of securities to US-based investors.

THREE
Insights

B efore starting the process of seeking financing in the form of equity financing by placing a minority stake in a qualified investor, you need to ask yourself whether you are truly ready. You must be committed to the process and prepared for what it means to become a publicly listed company. If you are not the ultimate decision-maker, you must have a mandate from the decision-makers, whoever they may be.

Do you have a mandate?

The days when private companies received equity funding in the form of minority positions from institutional investors in massive quantities are well behind us. An intelligent and enthusiastic entrepreneur can convince angels, family, and friends to join on such terms, but I can guarantee that the institutional crowd won't, no matter how good the business plan is. In many situations, institutional investors participating in a Series A have policies preventing them from leading investments in subsequent rounds.

CASE STUDY: When you don't have a mandate

Imagine you are the managing director of a fictional private company and you initiate a transaction and lead the project to take the company public. You feel that this makes sense for all shareholders and your management team. It is time to "professionalize" the board and the management team. You have worked with the SPAC sponsor team for almost six months on the plan to go public, have had countless meetings, done innumerable reviews, and run plenty of financial model iterations. Your company has spent hundreds of thousands of dollars on accountants and expert reports, as has the SPAC sponsor. When all parties are ready, and the valuation discussions kick in, it turns out that one influential shareholder is not happy with the overall transaction. As you might be able to guess, the deal can't be concluded and so it collapses. The lesson learned is that even if you are the managing director leading the project for the company, the controlling shareholder does not necessarily mandate you to take the company public at a certain valuation level.

The above scenario is a common occurrence, which is why it is imperative to know whether you have a clear mandate and to ensure that, internally, the majority and controlling shareholders agree with the plan to go public using a SPAC. Otherwise, the project is a waste of everyone's time and money.

To avoid this situation, you as a company owner must be ready to offer clear proof that you can take the company in that direction. If you're the founder of a company and you've taken money from venture capitalists, or if you've got some lenders, you again want to make sure that you have the green light to go ahead and seek the approval to go public. If you are part of the management team of a private company, in this case, it is usually a good idea to seek some early indications before incurring any expenses related to starting the process. SPAC sponsors will also want to ensure no negative controls could hamper the process before incurring expenses. Typically, going public may trigger a change of control clause. Understanding what you are and are not allowed to do will help you avoid headaches down the line.

Now, if you are the CEO, CFO, or project manager working for a company with a large group of shareholders, you must realize that you are not the only decision-maker. As such, you must get an explicit mandate from your board. You must also ensure that the board, in turn, has an explicit mandate from the shareholders.

In the case of a publicly listed company exploring the potential for a de-SPAC merger, shareholder approval will be required. In the case of a privately held company, going public is a "reserved matter" relating to the structure of your company that requires approval. Assuming this is the case, you need to understand the timeline and the process to get approval to go ahead. It makes sense to get approval in principle before getting started, instead of initiating the process, incurring expenses, and hiring service providers only to find out that, for one reason or another, the transaction may not be approved or can't go ahead. Given the number of such situations I have encountered, I recommend establishing the mandate early on and getting all possible objections put forward, instead of springing the idea of going public on decision-makers. Be ready to be questioned by institutional investors on your mandate.

Your service providers

When you enter negotiation with a SPAC, you will need at least three service providers: lawyers, bookkeepers, and auditors. If this is your first time negotiating a merger and a public listing, I highly recommend that you onboard an executive with experience in public companies as a project manager. They will ensure the process runs smoothly and can shepherd the various individuals in the correct direction. A project manager will also ensure that you are not entirely distracted from the main activity of running the business and that whatever obstacles you encounter throughout the process are quickly addressed and managed.

Regarding legal counsel, it should be straightforward to find a law firm. It pays to go with one experienced in dealing with de-SPAC mergers. The counsel used by the SPAC sponsors is particularly important, because it is these lawyers who handle the back-and-forth conversation with the SEC and clear their queries, as they are the driver of the process from the regulatory standpoint. If you have internal counsel familiar with the negotiation of mergers, then it is OK to rely on them, but this should be strictly from the perspective of reviewing the merger agreement and ensuring that your business interests are adequately protected.

In terms of bookkeepers, your accountants might be able to provide all the relevant information. Ideally, your company's audit report is ready and prepared according to IFRS standards. If you are a US company, most likely these will be adequate and can be immediately reviewed under the PCAOB standards. If your company is not incorporated in the US and you report under a different accounting standard, your book-keepers should be able to provide the information in a format that will allow the PCAOB audit to be conducted. Remember, the translation from your accounting and audit standards to a PCAOB audit standard will be tagged to your account, meaning that it is for your company to pay, not the SPAC or its sponsors. In any case, ensuring that your books are adequate and up to date is essential. Keep in mind that there is always a lot of demand for SPAC and merger auditors.

Accounting for an operating company is significantly more complex than for a SPAC, and it is the overall corporate structure of your business that will determine the cost of the audit. In the case that you have many operating companies in various jurisdictions organized as subsidiaries, the process is more complex and lengthier than if the business is simply grouped under a single US legal entity with only one level of accounting.

Typically, the cost of an audit for a private company gets put on the private company's account. Auditing the SPAC is generally straightforward because it has no real activity and simply maintains a cash balance inside a trust account; as such, it incurs only minor costs.

Depending on the level of merger activity, it may not always be easy to find a set of auditors who are competent in reviewing foreign entities, for example, and are also willing to take on the mandate. First, make sure that you have five or six alternatives if you intend to start the journey; reach out to them ahead of time and explore whether they can take on the challenge and the mandate; second, assuming they are willing to take it on, establish that they can commit to producing the PCAOB within the timeline required by the SPAC. Remember that the PCAOB audit is the gateway to closing the merger.

Whether you'll need an external project manager to drive the process depends on each company and its situation. Generally, it pays to have a professional executive oversee the process and manage the various streams across different counterparties (and time zones). The project manager is one of the most critical players in the project of taking your company public through a de-SPAC merger. Whether you insource or outsource the individual in charge, ensure they are appropriately mandated and can drive the process forward.

When you go public, you commit to making certain structural changes in your company; these changes imply greater transparency and reporting requirements going forward. Once listed, you'll have to provide quarterly reports and be questioned on these by analysts, so you are also committing to a greater level of communication with the world of investors and shareholders.

For these reasons, it makes sense to start thinking about who in your team will play the "investor relations" role and take the lead in facing investors and facilitating shareholder communication and interactions. Essentially, it's about who will be actively involved in the promotion of the company. If the talent is in-house, then it's simply a matter of repositioning the relevant individuals. You can also rely on the SPAC sponsor team, especially if they have a demonstrated track record; SPAC sponsors are typically well connected to the pool of investors.

Going public is an opportunity for you and your company to effect an upgrade to certain functions and to introduce enhancements in terms of staff and capability. These functions can also be outsourced, and different service providers can manage these aspects of your business economically and efficiently. Generally, all investor relations, corporate communication efforts, and investor-facing functions can easily be outsourced to specialized providers for companies with a low risk of trade secrets being leaked.

Choose the SPAC that fits you

The amount of capital available to merge with private businesses tends to vary over time; you can access the statistics by connecting with various information services. As all SPACs are publicly listed companies, you can obtain their information on the SEC website. The US exchanges comprise more than 12,000 listed companies.

With so much choice, how do you choose the right SPAC for your business? The key factors to focus on are:

- Team
- Size and makeup of shareholders
- Embedded restrictions and maturity
- Timeline

Team

Regarding the team, consider who is sponsoring this SPAC. First-time SPAC sponsors may not have the same level of experience as multi-SPAC sponsors. It is essential to look at the individuals that form part of the sponsors group of the SPAC. What is their track record? Is it their first SPAC? Their second? Are they serial SPAC issuers? In general, it pays to go with an experienced team, but they may not be as flexible when it comes to negotiation. A skilled team will typically have already determined what type of targets they want and potentially have a set of pre-defined sectors. As such, they may not be open to merging with your company if there is no natural fit. Although there cannot be a pre-arrangement or a pre-agreed set of specific targets for SPACs, it is likely that a SPAC team on their third or fourth deal will already have a good idea of broadly who they want to merge with.

Size

Regarding the size of the vehicle you are considering and its shareholder makeup, larger SPACs have more capital to deploy, but they also tend to attract higher costs. Conversely, if a SPAC has a minimal trust size, the company may have no capital left to operate once the redemptions are considered. Luckily, SPACs are transparent vehicles, and shareholders in the company can be easily identified or even contacted. Understanding their intentions ahead of time is part of the process of managing the redemption levels. It is beneficial to have shareholders who have long-term capital and are patient. Beware of SPACs that are almost exclusively funded with short-term hedge fund money. Often, these investors are only interested in the warrants issued by the SPAC and have no intention of remaining as a shareholder of the company; once the merger has occurred, they tend to redeem 100% of their original contributions every time.

Restrictions

Regarding the limitations of the SPAC, you must understand the restrictions that are imposed on what kind of business combination the SPAC can enter. There are no specific standards, but during 2020 and 2021 we saw the issuance of several SPACs where it was specified that they could not merge with companies located in China. In several cases, the sponsors had to explicitly state that they would not seek a business combination with a company located in Hong Kong, Macau, or China. Commonly, restrictions will concern sanctioned countries, such as Cuba or North Korea. This is where a project manager's assistance adds value by identifying early on some of the issues you may face during your negotiation with the sponsors of capital behind the SPAC you have chosen.

Time

Finally, you must carefully gauge how much time the SPAC has before it is forced to delist for regulatory reasons. Depending on the exchange, SPACs may have more or less flexibility about their expiry date. The expiry date has an impact on the transaction management process. The sponsors of a SPAC that is close to their expiry date will tend to be more flexible when negotiating, but this is a double-edged sword, as the prospect of being delisted may lead the sponsor to take more risks when it comes to the transaction. Conversely, SPACs that have recently gone public and have their full twenty-four months (or thirty-six months in some cases) remaining have a much longer runway and so are under less pressure to find a match quickly.

Managing the vote

An essential condition for a merger with a SPAC to succeed is that the trust investors approve it. The original investors in the SPAC commit capital upfront when the SPAC becomes public via an IPO, without knowing the object of the merger. As part of that commitment, they agree to lock up their capital for a period of anywhere between two and three years, with the expectation that the SPAC sponsor team will identify a great business—typically private and operating as an unlisted company—that the public cannot access as an investment opportunity. Essentially, these SPAC shareholders invest in a blind trust.

You and the SPAC sponsor then agree to merge your entities, making your business a publicly listed company and delivering the growth capital it needs. This step involves signing the business combination agreement (BCA), which is the merger agreement. Once signed, both parties will get to work to bring an S-4 statement (or an F-4 statement, if the companies are not registered in the USA) to the SEC. The S-4 statement is the document by which a merged pro forma company between a private business and a publicly listed vehicle is proposed to the SEC. The SEC's new listings team then assigns an inspector to review the statement and supporting documentation. There will be a few rounds of questions and answers between the SEC and the SPAC sponsors concerning various aspects of the transaction. The focus of these questions will range from valuation to the regulatory aspects of the transaction and even the history of how the two parties got to know each other, as well as the process by which they reached an agreement to merge.

Once the SEC is satisfied with the answers and agrees that the merger can go ahead, it will issue a statement of effectiveness; at that time, the merger is considered "effective" or that "the parties have gone effective." The green light is given, and the SPAC sponsors must return to their shareholders and call for a vote to approve the merger. The company typically has to give shareholders twenty calendar days' notice, at a minimum, to request a meeting of shareholders. At that meeting, they will vote on the resolutions related to the proposed merger. At this stage, the investors in the trust make two separate decisions. The first is whether they approve the SPAC merging with the target company. The second is whether they wish to remain a shareholder of the merged entity, now that they have the knowledge of what business the company is involved in going forward. They might prefer to redeem their capital, request a refund of the monies that they had initially invested, and walk away.

During 2023, there was a situation of high acceptance rates of mergers coupled with high rates of redemptions. The presence of structured arrangements and the late appearance of shareholders with different levels of rights and economics tend to have a significant impact on redemption rates. As mentioned in Chapter 1, these unique arrangements are often called PIPE transactions. They usually offer hybrid capital exposure to the publicly listed company, which frequently carries the right, but not the obligation, to purchase shares in the newly listed company at a significant discount on market rates. Therefore, even when an early investor, who forms part of the initial group of shareholders in the blind trust, finds the overall business attractive and is interested in financial exposure through shares, they will choose to redeem their capital and re-enter the deal via a PIPE transaction that may grant them the ability to purchase shares at a significant discount on the $10.

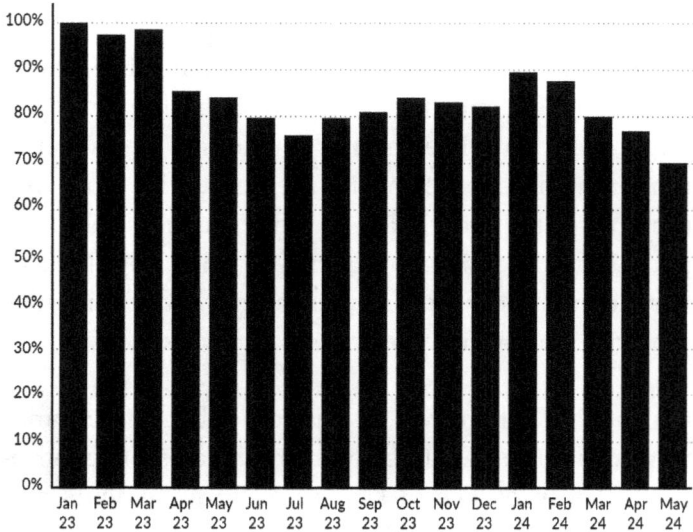

Redemption rates for the past twelve months
Graph by Daniel Mamadou-Blanco, data source: SEC

Timeline for the DREAMS protocol

Once you have identified a SPAC vehicle and reached an agreement with the SPAC sponsors, you can focus on the merger. You must be as efficient as possible and seek to complete the transaction as early as possible. As mentioned previously, delays are a feature of the process rather than an exception when doing a de-SPAC merger.

As part of managing the timetable, the first step is to engage the various service providers essential to the transaction management process. You may need local accounting services for each location, depending on whether you have regional operations in different jurisdictions. You will also need to identify local legal services and an audit firm to help with the PCAOB audit. As I indicated earlier, it can be challenging to find service providers willing to provide these services to non-US-based companies, and it is important to identify and compare the rates charged, as they can vary significantly. You will need to set aside a cushion of time for this process, as it could take several weeks to identify, select, and agree with the different providers. You'll need to establish how quickly they can clear the names of the two counterparties (the SPAC and your company), undertake conflict checks, and go through their respective new business committees before taking on your mandate. Once they start the work, converting your accounts from their existing accounting standards to US GAAP can take from four to twelve weeks. Only once that is done can the PCAOB audit begin. This happens more or less simultaneously with drafting the S-4/F-4 pro forma merger statement. How much time the entire process takes depends on your auditors' level of responsiveness.

Once the S-4/F-4 statement is finalized, it is submitted to the SEC, which will task one of its examiners with a first formal review. The S-4 statement is a filing required under the Securities Act to check whether the document aligns with the applicable disclosure and accounting requirements of companies publicly listed in US exchanges. The SEC is not interested in evaluating the financial merits of the transaction or whether the deal is suitable for investors. Instead, the SEC review focuses on whether the applicable accounting standards are met and whether the disclosure of information meets the standards of federal securities laws. A first review by the SEC could take four to six weeks, depending on how much backlog there is. A series of questions from the regulator typically accompany that first review, which implies that the S-4/F-4 statement needs to be revised and resubmitted to the SEC for further review. This process will continue until the SEC is satisfied with the answers submitted by the company. Upon the final review and approval, the SEC declares that the S-4/F-4 registration statement is effective. The merger can then proceed, assuming it is approved by the shareholders on both sides.

Typically, at this stage, the marketing for PIPE capital starts (in Chapter 4, we discuss in more detail why you should consider PIPE). At the same time, the original investors in the SPAC begin their due diligence on the target (your company). They will make a financial commitment to the transaction based on their appetite. The PIPE marketing can take three to four weeks, depending on the level of risk appetite of investors at the time. You should leave plenty of time to market the PIPE transaction.

When the financial commitments from strategic investors have been firmed up and contracts signed, and once the SEC has issued the statement of effectiveness, it is time to give notice of the extraordinary general meeting of shareholders of the SPAC and go into "closing mode." Typically, the SPAC needs to notify shareholders that the merger has become effective by calling for an extraordinary general meeting of shareholders and submitting the merger for approval by shareholders, giving them a minimum of twenty days' notice. The transaction closes once the vote has taken place and approval has been granted. Two days later, the newly merged company (MergedCo) starts trading on the relevant exchange. *Et voilà*—your company is now publicly listed.

FOUR

A Legal Perspective

As the shareholder and owner of a private company looking to go public with a SPAC, you will have to review many elements from a legal perspective. These can be distilled into four specific areas: valuation, net cash at close, lockup period, and management incentive scheme. In this chapter, we'll look at each of these in detail.

Valuation

The valuation of your company is one of the most critical factors. The figure you arrive at results from a direct negotiation between you, as a private company owner, and the SPAC sponsor team as the entity that brings cash and public listing to the table. Valuing your business is more complex than calculating the financial contribution that the SPAC makes to MergedCo, and you will need to value both the SPAC and your private business.

The SPAC value is essentially the cash contained in the trust multiplied by the expected redemption factor plus the amount of PIPE financing the sponsor expects to bring as part of the transaction. The redemption factor depends on the general market's risk appetite at the time and the quality of the target to be merged with the SPAC. For example, a SPAC with $200 million in cash in trust brings $200 million in value to the pro forma merged entity, assuming no PIPE and zero redemptions. This does not account for the interest accrued by the fixed-income securities in which the trust has invested during the lifetime of the SPAC. This interest is typically attributable to the shareholders and is reflected in the evolution of the SPAC's share price, which results in a visually pleasing stock price curve shaped as a straight upward line.

Valuing your private business is more complicated, and revenue-generating companies that belong to a specific activity sector are often valued using comparable observations from the market. Of course, all aspects of your operations should also be taken into account, such as your profits (if any), your market positioning, the pipeline of new orders, existing purchase or offtake contracts, and the value of your assets (both tangible and intangible). Explaining how to value private businesses is beyond the scope of this book, but there are plenty of other resources available for this purpose.

Net cash at close

In terms of cash at close, you need to be able to cover the expenses for the merger plus all the financial requirements of the business, both in terms of capital expenditure as well as operating costs, for at least twelve months. There is nothing worse than going public and then having to tap the markets shortly after for additional capital, unless there is a compelling reason to do so. You need to consider that once you are publicly listed, you will have to publish quarterly earnings reports and attend calls with financial analysts who will review the performance of the business and may also issue research reports. In addition, it is possible that the funding window for follow-on issues could remain closed for some reason, preventing MergedCo from looking to the markets for funding for a few months or even a year. As such, it is vital to make sure that the amount of cash the company receives upon closing the merger, net of all closing expenses, is sufficient for you to run your operations with no interruptions.

To negotiate the net cash at close, you should take the most conservative approach and assume that the redemptions on the SPAC are likely to be close to 100%. In this case, you cannot count on being able to extract any meaningful amount of cash from the trust. If the redemption levels are lower than expected, consider that a bonus. As the team turns its focus to getting the right amount of money for the business, PIPEs and structured capital arrangements come into play.

PIPE investment

The integration of a PIPE investment serves two purposes:

1. It is a signaling mechanism to show the other shareholders that the company's business is endorsed by an institutional investor who knows the sector and believes in the investment proposition at the stated valuation.

2. It is the easiest and most predictable way to manage the cash available after the merger.

You, as the owner of the private business, must insist on having a minimum cash amount at the close condition for the merger. Mergers cannot be reversed once they have been approved but having a minimum cash at close amount in the list of conditions for entering into the merger is an intelligent way to keep your options open. After all, your primary interest in the merger is more accessible financing due to the public nature of the company. As a private business owner, the cash at close condition gives you a way out of the merger if the SPAC sponsor team can't get the capital required for the business to function.

One of the reasons why many SPAC mergers fail is that the sponsors cannot get the amount of cash initially specified in the contract. This could be due to unrealistic expectations regarding the valuation of the combined entity. The PIPE is the valuation mirror that the market holds up to the parties to the merger.

Insisting on a high number for the cash at the close is a strategy some private company owners use. Still, you should remain open to renegotiating this number and adjusting it to the reality of the situation as and when the time to close arrives. You can also adopt the strategy of not imposing a minimum cash amount at close condition, but this could send the wrong signal to the market. For example, it might suggest that the parties are desperate to get the deal through irrespective of the redemption rate of the SPAC trust, and are not confident about the level of funds they can raise. A good SPAC project manager will help you read the market to identify the appropriate approach, but generally, the cash at the close is an excellent way to keep some options open instead of being forced to go ahead with a merger you may later regret.

Merger costs significantly impact the cash at close because they are taken directly from the amount of money raised (composed of the PIPE investment and the amount of cash not redeemed). However, the investment bankers that help raise the PIPE financing may be flexible and accept part of their compensation in shares of MergedCo.

Lockups

The market will view favorably transactions where the lockup period applies to everyone in the company and SPAC, including the SPAC sponsors and potentially PIPE investors. However, from time to time, concessions need to be made. It could be that PIPE investors are willing to come in under the condition of a shorter lockup period on their shares (or maybe no lockup at all). Managing the restrictions on the shares issued to PIPE investors is an essential point of negotiation that you must decide on early on, along with all the capital providers in the transaction.

An extended lockup period tends to be better for the share price performance, as it removes selling pressure from the market. Many PIPE investors will structure their investments so that their downside is limited. Still, their upside is monetized by selling the securities into which they can convert their PIPE instrument. Removing selling pressure should be a consideration when structuring the PIPE. Sudden drops in the price of SPAC shares, once they become effective, are often due to not having imposed a lockup period and restrictions on share sales, where the PIPE investors then dump their stock on the market the moment the shares can be publicly traded.

Management incentive scheme

Finally, as owner of a private company, you should insist on creating an incentive scheme for management. Going public through a SPAC merger does attract a certain amount of dilution and the inclusion of a PIPE also negatively impacts the shareholders. Some of these effects can be rebalanced by establishing an incentive plan designed to reward the initial shareholders of the private company with additional stock, depending on the company meeting accretive financial and operational milestones. It is a common and flexible mechanism used to attract and keep talent going forward.

Insurance

The next important legal point to check when engaging with a SPAC is the level of insurance coverage that the SPAC currently has to protect the board. As you transition to becoming a publicly listed entity, it is critical to cover the topic of directors and officers (D&O) insurance with the SPAC sponsors. As both entities end up becoming one, any legal action as a result of the merger will affect the entire board.

The typical coverage areas in terms of insurance are split into A, B, and C types. The A type, also called "Side A coverage," focuses on the individual directors and officers to personally shield them from lawsuits involving the management role. This is essential because, without it, the personal assets of the directors or individuals concerned could be at risk. It is unlikely that any director would agree to join the company board without evidence of Side A insurance coverage being in place.

Side B insurance relates to the company itself, covering any costs the company may have to pay for expenses incurred when the company indemnifies directors and officers for the costs of a lawsuit. Finally, Side C insurance covers the company when there are lawsuits related to securities, such as misrepresentation in financial statements.

I recommend having as comprehensive coverage as possible. It just makes sense. It also pays to ensure that these contracts are in place ahead of the merger. As the incoming party to the public company, you (the private business owner) will also want to understand the specifics regarding limits or any gaps in the coverage that the insurance company provides and whether there are deductibles. Will the company need to pay any out-of-pocket expenses before the insurance coverage kicks in? A specific list of exclusions is also good; dishonesty, other criminal acts, and existing liabilities tend to be excluded from Sides B and C coverage.

The list below summarizes the main points that should be covered under a standard D&O insurance package for a US publicly listed company:

1. Individual directors and officers:

   - Personal assets of directors and officers in case of a lawsuit

   - Legal fees, settlements, and judgments arising from alleged wrongful acts

   - Wrongful acts may include breach of duty, neglect, misstatements, or errors

2. The company itself:

   - Reimburses the company for legal costs and settlements if it indemnifies its directors and officers

   - Securities claims brought against it

3. Policy limits:

   - Specifies the maximum amount the insurer will pay for covered claims

   - Limits can be set per claim or policy period

   - Higher limits generally correspond to higher premiums

4. Retention or deductibles:

   - The amount the company must pay before the insurance coverage kicks in

- In other insurance policies, it is often described as a deductible

5. Policy period:

   - The length of time the policy provides coverage for, usually one year

   - Claims made during this period are covered, subject to the policy's terms and conditions

6. Exclusions:

   - Specifies situations or types of claims that are not covered by the policy

   - Common exclusions include fraud, intentional misconduct, and illegal compensation

7. Severability clause:

   - Ensures that the wrongful acts of one insured individual do not affect the coverage for other innocent insureds

8. Advancement of legal fees:

   - Allows directors and officers to have their legal fees paid by the insurer as they are incurred, rather than waiting for the claim to be resolved

9. Extended reporting period (tail coverage):

   - Provides coverage for claims made after the policy expires but relating to wrongful acts that occurred during the policy period

10. Worldwide coverage:

- Offers protection for claims brought against directors and officers in various jurisdictions worldwide

Trusted network

When millions of dollars are at stake, the issue of trust becomes more important. Don't jump into the capital-raising process without planning or a recommendation; otherwise, you might be ignored entirely, which is why raising capital can be arduous. Here are some tips on how to go about establishing a network of trusted parties, which will come in handy when you are raising capital.

It is essential to understand how the network of agents and stakeholders that participate in a merger with a publicly listed vehicle operates and who the main players are. As mentioned in the previous chapter, in terms of stakeholders, you have lawyers who act on each side of the transaction. Both you and the SPAC need legal advisers to ensure that the interests of each party are appropriately represented and realized. Next, you have the investment bankers, who essentially build the book of demand, initially for the SPAC IPO and then also for the de-SPAC merger; they can bring PIPE investors to the table and help manage the redemption process. The list of other service providers is long and includes accountants, insurance brokers, bookkeepers, proxy advisers, industry experts (especially if the private company operates in a highly specialized sector where technology is critical, such as biotech), investor relations specialists, etc.

The diversity of parties and their coordination is one of the reasons why executing a merger with a SPAC can become a complicated and complex process. It is also the main reason I recommend that you either designate a person in your organization to drive the process or enlist the services of a project manager experienced in de-SPAC mergers. The various stakeholders are all focused on absolute efficiency, given that there is a time limit to get the merger done, so generally, efficiency and trust come before cost considerations. An institutional investor is more likely to consider your company as a target if the connection has been made via a trusted party, or if you have been referred by a recognized player in the space. A completely cold approach could work, but you are unlikely to be treated with the same level of interest if there is no recommendation behind your introduction to an institutional investor. Institutional investors (or "instos" as they are called in the industry) tend to focus on the "do-ability" factor of the transaction: they will only invest their time (and their money) in engaging with parties that recognize the challenges of a merger, understand the timelines, and demonstrate the level of focus required to reach the finish line.

Entering a merger is an exercise in dispensing trust; the negotiation must be based on mutual respect and a desire to cooperate, establish a partnership, and forge a bond. Once the merger is done, the management teams of both parties must co-exist, even if only for the period that the shares are locked up. The typical board of a newly merged de-SPAC has individuals from both sides of the alley. It is the negotiation that determines the board composition, leading to the BCA being signed, so it is always best to connect with the different parties through introductions. Ask your project manager or SPAC banker to introduce you and provide referrals to the various service providers. This will ensure that your queries are well received, and the response rate will be higher than if you went ahead directly without any introduction.

Post-merger funding

Once you've become a publicly listed company, it is generally easier to raise capital—and the sources of capital differ. Usually, as a private company, you tend to bring in shareholders only from time to time; capital is typically raised by borrowing money from banks or specialty lenders. As a publicly listed company, the range of options for raising capital widens, including selling different types of securities to the public. This is one of the main attractions of a public listing. This additional functionality regarding issuance instruments must also be considered and valued, especially when negotiating the cash at close condition of the merger. You may want to be flexible on that condition and agree to a lower amount of cash at close, knowing that it will be easier to raise capital going forward as a listed company.

When CFOs of public companies require additional capital, they can pick up the phone and call their capital markets banker. At that stage, all they must negotiate is the level of dilution and discount to VWAP (volume weighted average price) of the listed stock over the previous ten days, and they can print an issue of shares. Listed companies also have access to more structured capital issuance instruments, such as equity lines of credit (ELOCS), which enable the issuing and selling of shares before raising capital through a forward-starting issuance of treasury stock. ELOCS have become relatively standard instruments routinely used by publicly listed companies. The other type of capital instruments issued are preferred shares. They are called "preferred" because they guarantee a dividend as a payment to be disbursed before making any dividend payment to ordinary shareholders. The advantage of issuing preferred shares in a company is that the voting rights of ordinary shareholders are not diluted.

PART TWO
A TRIED-AND-TESTED ROADMAP

I've done the groundwork for you. In this part of the book, you will discover that prestige, expansion, and sustainability are yours for the taking.

FIVE
The DREAMS Protocol

A s we learned in Part One, getting funding for a
business is a process, and obtaining good results
is not about luck but rather following the proper protocol and focusing on what matters to institutional
investors. After spending more than twenty years
scanning through business networks, identifying
companies with the potential to attract institutional
capital, and originate capital markets mandates, I
distilled my knowledge and experience to create the
DREAMS protocol. It is an easy-to-understand but
powerful approach that private businesses can follow
to position themselves in a way that will maximize
their chances of attracting equity capital from institutional investors.

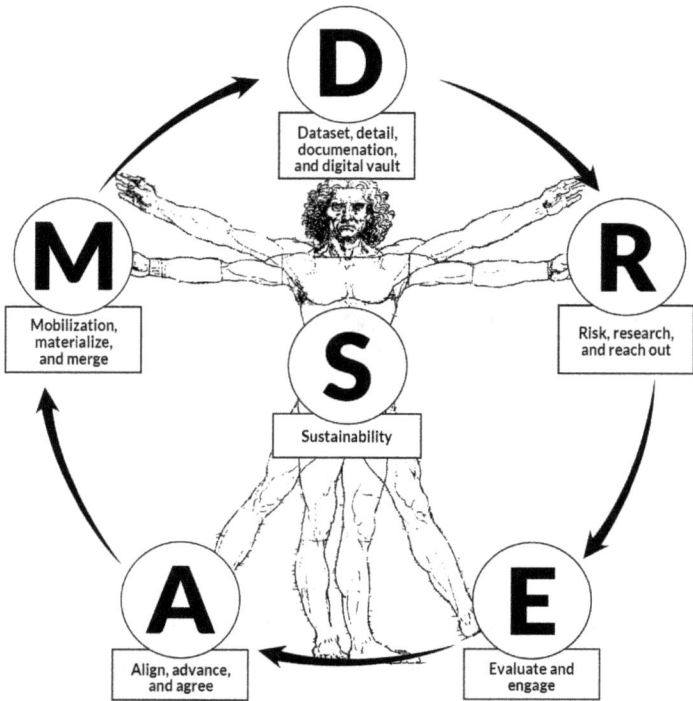

The DREAMS protocol

D: Dataset, detail, documentation, and digital vault

In this first step, the focus is on gathering and presenting all the relevant information required for an institutional investor to make an informed decision about investing in your business. For an institutional investor to be able to review your business thoroughly, this information must be adequately organized and, more importantly, it must be accessible in a way that allows a desktop review in the initial stage of the due diligence process. Note that this is not about creating a pitch deck or a product brochure. Often, I am presented with a lot of information that is not relevant to the decision to invest. You need a data package that can be shared with investors once they have signed a non-disclosure agreement (NDA). This data package should include:

- A teaser containing high-level information about the company and its business.

- An extensive management presentation that covers all aspects of the business, including the people behind it, the problems solved by the company, the products sold, the essential commercial relationships, a list of assets, existing borrowings, the brands and patents owned, plus any other relevant data.

- The three essential financial documents: a balance sheet, cash flow statements, and an income statement, available separately.

- A financial model with revenue projections for the next five years. The assumptions used in this model need to be clearly articulated, and constructed in a way that means they can be easily changed so that various simulations can be run. The sources supporting these assumptions, which must be official, also need to be documented.

NDAs

You will need a specially crafted NDA if your business is heavy in industrial secrets. Institutional investors, and SPACs in particular, tend to have special NDAs with clauses preventing their cash in trust from being exposed to any claim, and they will likely have no flexibility around that part. Beyond this, standard terms tend to include a maturity of one to two years and a non-circumvention clause designed to prevent bypassing by one party. Typically, the NDA should not contain any indemnification clause.

A note about negotiating and signing NDAs: I have seen situations where the target company has dragged its feet negotiating the NDA or has imposed drastic conditions such as reporting requirements placed on the recipient of the information. In one extreme case, the target company even requested the placement of a monetary deposit by the potential investor as a condition to open the data room. Remember that institutional investors receive hundreds of investment proposals every month, and the key to successfully getting on their radar is to make it easy for them to agree to commit analytics resources in the first instance while also maintaining the integrity of your proprietary information. The bottom line is: don't make signing an NDA with an investor overly tricky. If you reach that stage, there will be a time to get tough in the negotiation process. However, the signing of the NDA is not the right time for this. The goal is to engage the investor and get them to spend time reviewing your proposal instead of someone else's. Still, the NDA is an essential psychological moment because it is the first agreement with each other that both parties will sign, and it will send signals to each party about the approach and behavior of the other when it comes to protocol and agreements.

Once the information and documentation are ready, you must upload everything to a digital vault called a VDR (virtual data room). I have no strong view concerning the best VDR software; I have seen deal information shared by simply sending a USB drive, and I have seen expensive data room applications with high functionality. You can also use solutions like Google Drive or Dropbox. There is no real advantage or disadvantage in using one or the other; the choice of VDR application does not increase your chances of getting an investment. What matters is getting the correct information into the right hands, clearly ordered and in an easily digestible format—this *does* increase your chances of investment. You don't want a massive, complicated data room with thousands of chapters at this stage; your aim is to get the institutional investor to sign an NDA, enter the VDR, and review the information. They can then conclude whether the company is investable from their perspective and decide to do a deep dive.

To finalize the first step of the DREAMS protocol, you need to get your teaser and NDA ready to be shared by email and have the VDR up and running. Once this is done, you can move on to the next step.

R: Risk, research, and reach out

The biggest concern of institutional investors is risk management, which is why this is its own step in the DREAMS protocol. Way too often, business owners are keen to present the economic feats of the business and fail to recognize that institutional investors are, by definition, risk averse. Directors on boards of publicly listed companies have personal liability and so are concerned about risk management, even if that fact is not obvious. For this reason, as a company, you need to be actively managing the various risks that affect your business. If you don't have a clear risk management policy, now is the time to create one, as it will be high on the due diligence list of institutional investors.

You must also research which institutional investors are more likely to agree to listen to your story. As we've learned, the SPAC market is the most fertile hunting ground for institutional investors. There are many pre-conceived ideas about SPACs, but they are the purest expression of an investor because they are:

- **Of an institutional nature:** A publicly listed company with a professional board mainly composed of independent directors.

- **Cash-rich:** Due to the minimum market capitalization requirements set by the regulators, SPACs need to have cash on their balance sheet. That money is typically locked up in a trust account, earning base interest until the management of the SPAC finds a target and agrees to deliver that cash to the target as part of the BCA.

- **Looking to invest soon:** SPACs have a finite lifespan and need to enter into a business combination within a maximum of three years (for a Nasdaq-listed SPAC).

- **A fundamental minority equity investor:** SPACs rarely represent more than 20% of the combined entity once the merger occurs. They do not require or request control. Instead, when they enter into a merger, SPACs behave as minority interest equity investors.

Draft a list of the SPACs you wish to contact and sort this list by expiry date, from soonest to latest. SPACs typically have the flexibility to merge with almost any type of business, even if they prefer a particular sector. SPACs close to their expiry date tend to be more flexible on the nature of the business they merge with. Your focus at this stage should be on determining which SPACs are likely to consider your company a valid investment for their merger aspirations. As most information about SPACs is public, it is easy to evaluate how much capital is available for your particular sector. Information about the decision-makers is also public, making it a breeze to connect and engage with them and show them your proposal—this is the next step.

It is essential to know where to spend your time. If you have a project manager or a CFO, task them with identifying the right pool of investors who can eventually be approached with an offer. The best way to determine who has capital to deploy is to go to the SEC website and review all the companies that are focused on acquisitions; these are companies quoted on the exchange that have a timeline before they need to delist, and that have announced they are looking for a target to merge with. This part of the process can be tedious, but it is crucial. It is one area where getting in touch with a specialist in de-SPAC mergers pays off. You can do this job by yourself, but a specialist and sector professional will radically cut the time required to do the research. At any one time, several billion dollars of capital are available but locked up in various trusts across tens of listed companies looking to enter a merger where they would take a non-controlling position and provide capital (in the form of equity) to a private business that they like. It is in that pool of investors that the DREAMS protocol works best. These companies are focused exclusively on deploying capital into private companies. Some entities have restrictions concerning the sector they will enter into, but generally, they have a lot of flexibility.

In the risk, research, and reach-out stage, your aim is to identify which companies have the capital to deploy, how much capital is locked up in trust, and when this capital needs to be deployed. Logically, the companies that are close to expiry without a matched target are likely to be more eager to enter into a business combination with a private company than those that have recently done an IPO and have twenty-four or thirty-six months before they have to delist. Focusing on companies with just a few months left on their shelf and that are generally agnostic from a sector perspective is a great approach.

Once you have your list of likely targets, you have completed the second step of the DREAMS protocol.

E: Evaluate and engage

Now that you have a list of potential investors, it is time to evaluate and then engage with your SPAC options. You must first assess each SPAC on the list, looking at the track record of the individuals who manage each particular SPAC entity. Some teams will be experienced, and this may be their third or fourth SPAC deal transaction. These tend to be specialists in bringing companies from the private realm to the public markets. There is an advantage to working with experienced people who have a track record in dealing with regulatory authorities. During the evaluation step, you will find that some of these SPACs work within a particular theme or specialization, or have a specific focus, which may match well with the concept of your company.

This third step is also where you, as the owner of the potential target, need to define what you are ready to put on the table and your minimum requirements for entering into a BCA. Essentially, you need a clear idea of the deal you are prepared to offer.

Then, it is time to engage by physically (and electronically) connecting with one or more members of the board of the SPAC (or SPACs) identified as a good fit in the previous step. You can reach out to the CEO. Typically, their name will be on the front cover of the S-1 statement filed with the SEC, along with a mailing address and sometimes a telephone number. In some instances, you may even get an email address. Generally, these companies also provide contact details on their website. Alternatively, your project manager should be able to reach out to either the CFO or the company's CEO directly. You could also look at which investment bank brought the SPAC public and reach out to them, naming the specific SPAC you want to get in contact with.

There are many ways to reach the SPAC sponsors, including connecting on social media, using specialized professional social media platforms such as LinkedIn, and asking to be connected with people. If possible, get someone to introduce you. Send a short introduction message with your teaser and your NDA attached to the relevant individual, asking them to reply if they are interested in knowing more about your business. Remember that we are all bombarded with emails and messages daily, and it may take days before you get a response. However, rest assured, motivated investors will get back to you.

A: Align, advance, and agree

We have now reached the fourth step in the DREAMS protocol, where you align interests and advance the process to culminate in an agreement in principle on a deal. This step is crucial, as it is when you decide to go public as a company owner. This decision is almost always irreversible. This step only occurs after a SPAC prospect has expressed interest in engaging with and signing the NDA.

Shortly after reaching out to motivated SPAC sponsors, you may get expressions of interest from some of these parties. To access the complete information, they would have to come back to you either with a signed NDA or perhaps with a request to sign their own version. Some SPACs can be particular regarding the wording of the NDA, and they may not have the flexibility to use any format other than theirs, which their own legal counsel would have prepared.

In this phase, once NDAs are out of the way, the dialogue will intensify, as the SPAC sponsor seeks to understand your business better and decides whether your company constitutes a valid target for their vehicle. This is where you grant them access to the

VDR that you created in the first step. You must also be ready to get on video conference calls and participate in desktop due diligence sessions. Depending on the nature of your business, physical due diligence may also be required, with the SPAC sponsor either conducting these sessions themselves or sometimes using third parties. During this part of the process, you need to show absolute responsiveness and openness concerning your business. Don't worry; the NDA protects you.

Now is also when the two parties seek alignment on the merger terms. As with any negotiation process, it's helpful to define the high-level objectives and goals using a draft term sheet. The gaps between the parties' positions will become apparent and both sides will work to close the bid offer on all or most of the outstanding negotiation points to hopefully reach a meeting of minds and lay out the final conditions of the overall merger. Some of the critical items during this step are the valuation of the company, the cash that will remain in the company after the close of the merger (and after all fees have been paid), and the lockup period for the company shares.

During this phase, you'll also agree on the composition of the board of MergedCo. Typically, you would retain some of the existing board members of the listed company, and you would bring your own board. You may also decide to bring in additional professional help by hiring a CEO. This step of the DREAMS protocol is where all these crucial details get hammered out.

As we introduced earlier, a good way for you to keep some optionality in the process is to impose some form of minimum cash condition at close. This is a necessary clause that stipulates that unless you end up with that minimum amount of cash as a company upon close, you are not committed to the merger. The implication is that irrespective of the level of redemptions in the trust, it is guaranteed that if you go ahead with a deal, the company will be adequately funded. The minimum cash at close must cover all expenses the SPAC has accrued to merge into MergedCo. It should also provide the base capital to fund several months of growth to fulfill the business objectives, including the pipeline your company has set for itself. Negotiating this point is when the costs of the merger are disclosed and become transparent to all parties. The parties will negotiate and sometimes renegotiate all the costs involved in closing the merger, including any deferred fees that may be owed to the various service providers involved. It is vital that the cost structure is palatable, and sustainable, and does not hamper the business going forward. This is also the moment to negotiate the management incentives.

In a nutshell, this step is where the deal is crafted, negotiated, and agreed upon, including the level of dilution the different parties will endure. The alignment phase should culminate in an agreement in principle, which can be framed as a Letter of Intent (LOI). The LOI can be binding or not, depending on how far the parties have progressed in reaching alignment. The LOI will likely be publicly announced; like all publicly listed companies, SPACs have a continuous public disclosure obligation, and signing an LOI is a significant and material event and so must be disclosed. External legal counsel should be hired to review the LOI. If what is being considered is a BCA, then the involvement of legal counsel is essential. Do not sign a BCA without legal counsel.

M: Mobilize, materialize, and merge

This is the operational step of the DREAMS protocol and is the immediate precursor to the actual merger itself. If you have reached this step, you will have signed either an LOI or a BCA, and you have a timeline and potentially a deadline by which the merger needs to have been completed. At the beginning of this step, you need to formally engage your execution team, including external service providers. Auditors must be independent and hired externally. They will audit your accounts according to PCAOB standards. It is often the same case for legal counsel, and they need to be involved to help you review all of the agreements. The rest of the execution functions can be internalized if you feel comfortable and confident in managing the process and coordinating all parties. During this step, the PIPE marketing also starts (and ends).

The audit

Let us dwell for a moment on the topic of the audited accounts. As we learned earlier, being able to successfully undertake—and pass—a PCAOB audit is the main gating item for a successful merger with a US-listed SPAC. The audited accounts need to be delivered on a pro forma basis, hand in hand with the audited accounts of the SPAC. Typically, a SPAC has a simple audit process because it is simply a cash shell, a company with no activity. For your company, the target, things will be more complicated and a few things can extend the process—the existence and number of foreign subsidiaries and operating companies that sit under your parent company, for example. Accounts drafted in a language other than English can also prove to be an obstacle to a successful merger, as translation in terms of both language and accounting standards will be required.

Once the PCAOB audit is done and finalized, the SPAC sponsor can produce an S-4/F-4 registration statement to submit to the SEC for review. Typically, PIPE investors enter the transaction once the merger has been announced, ie, the target has been identified. At this time, institutional investors who are familiar with your sector should also be approached with an investment of a specific size (which can be anything). Typically, the capital that comes via PIPE tends to have preferential terms to those that the investors in the SPAC at $10 have. The presence of these instruments at the capitalization table partly drives the level of redemptions from the SPAC shareholders. Who wants to buy stock at $10 when others are getting a discount?

There are often optionality discounts, which can be structured in the form of loans. As such, it is vital to understand the level of dilution and the impact on the company's financial health going forward that each instrument coming into the deal provides. Any additional capital instrument embedded in the transaction (such as PIPE) must also be disclosed and included in the submission document. The SEC is mainly concerned with ensuring proper disclosure of dilutive capital instruments (PIPE arrangements) introduced into MergedCo as part of the deal.

After the audit, the SEC will review whether the company is fit and proper to be listed on the US Securities Exchange, as described earlier. When a SPAC goes public and lists on the Nasdaq, for example, it cannot have maintained any substantive prior discussion with any target with which it intends to merge. In other words, a SPAC cannot be set up for a specific target based on an agreement that has occurred before the creation of the SPAC. Once the SEC is satisfied and has issued a statement of effectiveness, the merger is effective. The SPAC sponsor must then call for an extraordinary general meeting of shareholders in order for them to vote. It is at that vote that the shareholders decide whether to approve the merger and then if they wish to keep their investment in the trust or redeem their capital.

Managing cash at close

During the SPAC boom period of 2020 to 2023, it was common to see lots of mergers being approved but, at the same time, all the investors redeeming all or most of their cash. Remember that the original SPAC investors are unaware of what business will ultimately be brought into the listed company. During 2022 and 2023, the average amount of cash that was not redeemed and remained in the trust after the vote was 5%. This is an important lesson that you cannot rely on the trust size as an indicator to assess how much cash you will receive at close. If a certain amount of cash at close is needed, it is essential to ensure that additional capital is committed at the time of the merger. Ideally, this capital should come from investors who understand your sector because it is their investment that will validate the transaction from both a valuation perspective and a financial projection perspective. It is not an essential condition to have a PIPE investor in the deal, but it is recommended to bring one such investor in. PIPEs are designed to provide credibility to the merger and to validate the valuation of your company based on which the SPAC enters the merger.

The other way to manage the cash at close condition is through the establishment of NRAs (non-redemption agreements); these are a type of agreement between the SPAC sponsors and some of the shareholders of the trust, where the shareholders pledge not to redeem their contribution to the trust, in exchange for getting a discount in the form of additional sponsor shares, or warrants.

S: Seek sustainability

Attracting the attention of institutional investors is dependent on showing how well prepared you are, as a company, to face the challenges of operating under the scrutiny of public investors and to the standards of exchange-listed companies. As of 2024, more than half of the world's stock exchanges require each listed company to produce a sustainability report. Judging by the direction in which the world is going, eventually, this requirement will be extended to private businesses. As a business owner, you should be ready, even if it seems that you are ahead of time. In fact, this is an area where you can differentiate yourself. There is nothing to lose and everything to gain by demonstrating your awareness of the sustainability of your business. Companies that generate sustainability reports are considered transparent, accountable, and inclusive. A sustainability reporting initiative shows that the management is committed to continuous improvements because such a report requires setting goals and measuring performance-driven objectives, including reducing the business's carbon footprint.

From an operational perspective, starting such an initiative internally does not represent a significant burden. However you, as a business owner or senior manager, need to familiarize yourself with the organizations and frameworks that form the base of sustainability efforts today, namely the Global Reporting Initiatives (GRI), the International Sustainability Standard Board (ISSB), and the recently introduced Task Force on Climate-related Financial Disclosure (TCFD). You must demonstrate your understanding of how your business aligns with and responds to the demand from society for a cleaner and less unequal world.

There is no doubt that sustainability reporting impacts financing, as it necessitates discipline on the risk management front. We have already highlighted how risk management (part of the second step of the DREAMS protocol) can affect a business's financial performance and resilience. A company that can efficiently manage its sustainability risks will be perceived as less risky overall and, therefore, more attractive as a potential investment opportunity. Institutional investors have also been increasing the amount of funds channeled to sustainable companies and businesses with strong ESG (environmental and social governance) credentials, and the terms offered to sustainable companies are demonstrably better. The market for sustainable finance products is also growing, and your company will benefit from better access to capital if you can show a focus on sustainability risk management.

In conclusion, there is no debate about the long-term value creation that stems from addressing ESG issues and managing sustainability risk in your business. Institutional investors look for profitable companies that can also demonstrate a sustainable business model for the long term. By highlighting your sustainability credentials, you show that your company is aware of its position within society and that you make this a focus point; this acts as a silent filter for an increasing number of institutional investors.

SIX

Objections

In this chapter, I'll review some common misconceptions about and objections to pursuing de-SPAC mergers, and explain either why these are wrong, or how you can overcome them.

Too small to go public

There is no minimum size for a business wanting to merge with a SPAC, so don't sell yourself short by thinking your company doesn't have the scale.

If you are in expansion mode, it doesn't matter what size you are to start with; what matters is that going public will enable you to grow faster. It will provide you with a currency that will allow you to acquire your competitors and expand your market to other verticals and countries. It will give you the recognition and the prestige of being listed. It will also enable you to explore broader initiatives and unlock new business opportunities. That is the meaning of expansion. In that sense, arguably, if you consider your business small, you have even more reason to try and go public as it will help you to grow faster instead of staying as you are.

The different exchanges impose minimum market capitalization requirements, and in the case of the Nasdaq Global Exchange, that number currently stands at US$50 million at issuance.[13]

Since 2015, more than fifteen companies with valuations below US$100 million obtained funding from the SPAC market, including NewGenIvf (US$50 million), Peck Electric (US$53 million), VivoPower (US$53 million), and Jet Token (US$73 million).[14] The SPAC market is ultra-flexible when it comes to valuation, so as a private company owner (or managing director), never assume that the business is too early or too small to use this avenue for raising capital.

There are plenty of publicly listed companies with relatively small market capitalizations. They are doing absolutely fine. Their businesses are sustainable. The fact that they are publicly listed gives them an advantage when seeking additional financing and expansion opportunities.

When you look at the minimum trust size of a SPAC, it begins at $25 million. However, what is important is the valuation at which the transaction gets done and how much cash at close is generated for the benefit of the newly merged entity. When you look at the companies that currently trade on the Nasdaq market, you've got market caps as low as $15 million. The only limitation is that if your MergedCo has a market cap below $25 million, the exchange regulator may require you to either increase the capitalization or delist.[15]

For a small or medium-sized business, there are many advantages to merging with a SPAC to become public. Besides accessing the capital you require to power up the business, being listed means you can provide liquidity for your shareholders. Going public creates a liquid market for shares that may have been locked up in private hands for a long time. It allows all your early investors, angels, founders, friends and family, and even employees to monetize their investments. If you have a relevant employee incentive scheme in place, it also helps you retain your top talent by offering a path for employees and partners to share in the company's success.

Being publicly listed enhances your company's credibility and increases its visibility. This can be particularly useful when competing with more prominent entities; you may be able to attract business and contracts you might not have had access to as a private business. Some entities could decide to deal with you merely because you're a publicly listed company— it makes your company appear more trustworthy. Being public also enables you to diversify your funding sources. When faced with two businesses, one private versus one publicly listed, assuming they are the same size, the publicly listed company tends to be favored and will be better received by banks and other lenders. This is simply because a publicly listed company is more transparent to the market. Listing provides additional flexibility and can lead to greater financial stability, especially when the markets are rough. Finally, it can also attract some form of coverage by research analysts, which helps raise the company profile and provides valuable feedback to the management.

Too expensive

One common misconception is that merging with a SPAC to go public is too expensive. This is incorrect. Before passing judgment on this topic, you need to assess the cost of taking your company through the process of merging with a SPAC. In doing so, your focus should not be on how much it costs to close the SPAC, but on how all the merger expenses will be settled because, as the target private company, you will have to pay your share of the costs accrued during the process. This will be the amount you must pay your accountants and auditors.

How you settle these expenses is more important than the size of them. It has become an industry practice to pay the bulk of deferred expenses through shares and proceeds upon the de-SPAC merger instead of using upfront cash. You should look to your SPAC sponsor partners to ensure that as much of the cost as possible is deferred to the deal closure and settled with the proceeds generated from the merger. This means that what you should focus on when assessing how "expensive" the merger is, is the crucial point of the net cash at close that the company will receive once all expenses have been paid.

The expenses for the merger are usually wholly transparent and known to everyone involved in the process. As such, it is possible to reach an understanding and agreement on what the expense account will look like upfront before closing the transaction. This should be negotiated before signing the BCA. As the adage goes, "It takes money to make money." In this case, no SPAC is "too expensive," especially if shares are used to settle the expenses. Of course, you should manage these expenses and insist that service providers provide a cap on their estimates. You also want to ensure that you obtain estimates ahead of time and that all of these points are carefully reflected in the LOI and the BCA signed by the parties.

It will take too long

Another misconception about merging with a SPAC to raise capital is that the time spent closing the deal is too long. How fast the merger closes depends on how responsive and prepared the two parties are; whether the books have been audited; and whether the information about the company is up to date. If your team is focused and you have the right advisers, the process can be quick and smooth and should not interrupt the company's day-to-day activities.

Remember, every SPAC has a stated expiration date, so its sponsor is generally motivated to close a deal as quickly as possible. It is incumbent upon the target to be responsive and provide all the information relevant to the merger.

The SEC revision times are one of the factors that cannot be controlled. The time required for an AGM (Annual General Meeting) for the SPAC shareholders to vote on the transaction is at least twenty calendar days. However, with proper planning and using the DREAMS protocol to identify funding, a SPAC transaction could take four to six months. The idea that a SPAC merger takes too long is a myth; where this is the case, it is often due to a lack of responsiveness on the part of the private company.

If your deal is planned correctly and you've followed the DREAMS protocol, you will have your documentation ready and a team with a project manager handling all potential issues on your behalf. Or you can simply hire a project manager and an adviser for your SPAC; you need somebody skilled and experienced in the execution of merger mandates. The process of merging with the SPAC therefore ought to be short, and is the most efficient way to bring millions of dollars in financing into your company.

I will lose control of my business

Another fear of private company owners is that as "merger targets" they will lose control of the business if they go public.

This is an imaginary dragon. When the target enters into a merger with a publicly listed cash vehicle like a SPAC, the target ends up with the majority stake in MergedCo. As a private business owner, you will retain control if you maintain a significant ownership stake below 50%. This gives you the power to elect board members, you will approve all critical decisions, and, more importantly, you can shape the direction of the company going forward. Being publicly listed also enables you to establish a dual share structure, if that's what you want. Having two classes of shares is a way to retain control of the board even if you own less than 50% of the company, via a split between voting rights versus holdings.

With this control, you can establish a strong board of directors. Often, the board of MergedCo will shed and do away with members of the board of the SPAC; the pre-merger SPAC board members, especially experienced sponsors whose primary business is to bring companies public, will likely move on to their next project. You want directors who share your vision and will support your leadership, but remember that most of the board will need to be made up of independent directors. Provided you have a loyal and competent board, you can steer the company's direction going forward, even if you have less than 50% ownership.

Finally, one of the best ways to retain control of your company is to forge a strong relationship with the key shareholders and other stakeholders. There are different ways to structure the agreements in a publicly listed company. This essentially involves establishing a key shareholders agreement, where you specify the obligations and rights of various shareholders. In this, you can include provisions that set rules for deciding how to vote on critical issues.

The share price will drop

SPACs have attracted a lot of negative headlines because of share prices dropping once MergedCo begins trading. The causes of poor share price performance are multiple, but it is fair to say that once the company trades as a single merged entity, the market provides an immediate reflection of the value; if the share price drops, it is because there are more sellers than buyers of the stock. This is one of the main reasons you must team up with professionals and carefully manage the de-SPAC merger process.

In the current market, the difference between successful versus unsuccessful SPACs tends to be the team and the sponsor managing the transaction. Supply and demand of the paper on offer are greatly affected by the amount of structured capital, warrant, or options, and discounts on the $10 share price agreed with PIPE investors. This is why it is essential to design lockup provisions and limit the amount of structured capital that forms part of the transaction. It is also vital to bring in long-term shareholders who share the vision and plan to stay invested in the transaction for years to come. Limiting the participation of hedge funds and other short-term investors or "hot money" in the transaction is another consideration, and doing a smaller deal with a more modest and realistic transaction is better than trying to hit as high a valuation number as possible. The size of the trust is also a factor. The bigger the trust, the bigger the transaction and the valuation, but it also means higher expenses, leading to an increased likelihood of poor price performance in the aftermarket.

The demerger process also needs to be handled appropriately by the investment bankers and sponsors. They must create an environment where there will be more demand and less supply the moment the shares are trading freely on the stock exchange, and not the other way around. To achieve this, they must ensure that the investor appetite is not satisfied in one go. They must leave room for additional demand that can be filled by the investors, who then go to the open market to buy more shares. Independent research about the company is essential here, as it objectively evaluates the company and its value. If you get all of this right and have a team that looks at the overall transaction beyond the merger, the result will be a great post-de-SPAC merger price performance.

SPACs have a terrible reputation

There are many examples of high-quality businesses that have gone public through SPACs. Two good examples are DraftKings and MP Materials. SPACs' reputation as shady instruments is dated, and the financial press tends to focus on the negative cases and pay less attention to the successes (see Appendix 2).

SPACs are not at all dangerous, and they have gained a lot of popularity in recent years as an alternative route for companies to go public—they are more common than the financial press would have you believe. Some of the reasons why SPACs are popular is because the process is faster than the traditional IPO route and there is less uncertainty around pricing and market conditions. When it comes to complex businesses, which is common among private companies, SPACs are an attractive option because if you want to sell your story, the traditional IPO route can be difficult. For example, foreign companies with complex ownership and corporate structures, which are common in certain parts of the world, such as Asia, can be challenging to market through a standard IPO roadshow. They are much better suited to go public by merging with a SPAC.

The returns on the SPAC generally can be high, so shareholders like it. When teaming up with a SPAC, you typically inherit an experienced management team, which is handy when navigating the regulatory environment that affects publicly listed companies.

Though there are of course risks, SPACs are not dangerous, and your focus should be on the reputation of the sponsor team, which can enhance the reputation of the private companies that merge with them.

Here are just a few well-known companies that went public through mergers with SPACs:

- MP Materials started trading on the NYSE as the result of a merger with Fortress Value Acquisition Corp ("FVAC") in November 2020 in a $1.47 billion deal.

- Lionsgate Studios became public through the merger with Screaming Eagle Acquisition Corp in a $4.6 billion deal in May 2024.

- Grab Holdings went public through a merger with Altimeter Growth Corp in a $40 billion deal in April 2021.

Not an American company

If you are not a US-based company, and your operations are not carried out in the US, this doesn't mean you cannot merge with a US-listed entity. Quite the contrary. When you look at the stats, in 2023, 826 foreign companies were listed on the Nasdaq. That represents 23%. With $23 trillion of market capitalization, it is access to capital that motivates companies to list in the US.[16] The numbers fluctuate, but the US exchanges offer compelling reasons for international companies to list with them. The US capital markets are the deepest in the world and provide access to a large pool of investors and capital. They are also some of the best regulators, so being listed in the US increases your visibility and reputation. This provides the potential for higher valuations, and the markets are more liquid. A US listing implies that you adhere to the US securities laws and regulations, which include the Sarbanes-Oxley Act and the Foreign Corrupt Practices Act. The fact that you have the SEC as a watchdog will increase investor confidence in your company, making it easier to raise capital going forward. For all these reasons, it makes sense for your company to pursue listing in the US even if your operations are not carried out there.

The typical ways to get a non-US company listed are either direct listing by merging with a SPAC or via an American Depository Receipt (ADR), which is an avenue available to companies already listed in their own countries. If you own a company that is listed in your jurisdiction, you can decide to go down the ADR path. Alternatively, you can pursue a direct listing. Some well-known foreign companies that are listed in the US are Shopify and Toyota; these both meet several criteria that enable a dual listing process. Understanding and meeting these criteria is what this book aims to help you do.

Fear of takeovers

As the owner of a private company, you might feel secure in the knowledge that it's unlikely that an external actor will come and take over your business. If you lose your business, it will probably be due to lenders' repossession of the company's assets rather than a hostile action by external shareholders. When you're publicly listed, there is a real risk of this happening. Corporate raiders may try to take over a company that is publicly listed. However, exchanges have anti-takeover rules that regulate how and when this can occur. Realistically, what is likely to happen when you go public by merging with a SPAC is that you, as the original owner of the private business, will own a significant stake in the new company, typically anywhere between 65% and 75%. Such a sizable controlling position means it would take a considerable effort from a corporate raider to take over your company.

Once you become publicly listed, you can take a series of measures to avoid being taken over by corporate raiders. Your legal department will be able to craft the relevant defense mechanisms that will make the company less attractive as a target to be acquired without the consent of the board of directors. "Poison pills," for example, are a type of shareholder right that makes it expensive for a corporate raider to acquire a controlling stake. Once the poison pill is triggered, existing shareholders can obtain a discount when buying additional shares, which would diminish the effectiveness of a corporate raid. Golden parachutes for executives can be considered another form of poison pill that somewhat softens the blows of a corporate raider attack.

You can also create a staggered board; this is a board structure that allows for several classes of members, each with multiyear terms. Staggered boards make it difficult for corporate raiders to replace the entire board and gain control of the company.

Supermajority voting provisions are another defense mechanism that can be embedded in the structure of MergedCo; they require certain thresholds to be met before a takeover can be approved, making the exercise difficult for an external corporate raider to implement.

Over time, and after subsequent capital-raising exercises, your position will be diluted. That is when and how you may open yourself to a situation where your company could be taken over. However, as it is unlikely that your ownership will be diluted in the first few years of your business's existence as a publicly listed company, this shouldn't be a concern when merging with a SPAC.

Disclosure of executive compensation

It is good corporate governance for a publicly listed company to disclose the compensation of its top executives. That means the CEO, the CFO, and the key management personnel. In most countries nowadays, this is required of all publicly listed companies through regulation. Typically, this disclosure is included in the 10-Q and 10-K forms, which cover elements such as the base salary, bonuses, stock options, pensions, and all other benefits and deferred compensations.

A publicly listed company must also have a compensation committee and explain the philosophy by which it remunerates and rewards its executives. This is positive because it aligns the interests of the share-holders with those of the company's management. As a growing private company, it is a process you may want to implement early; the topic will surely come up when you ask for a loan or seek to raise capital as a private company because potential investors will ask these questions. They will want to know the compensation of the executives and the founders, and whether you are drawing a salary. They will then compare that with market practice in your sector and industry. The philosophy that you must embrace is that transparency is a good thing and does not create any additional obstacle to raising capital.

Transparency and accountability enable shareholders and prospective investors to make the right decision when voting on compensation packages. In the 10-K statement, a compensation discussion and analysis should explain the basis on which the compensation is granted to the various executives in the form of a table with a breakdown, a split of salary versus bonus, options, and other performance-related remuneration methods. It goes over the list of key management members and personnel. Addressing this point early on, even if you are still a private company, helps improve the sustainability of the business and leads to better practice from a governance point of view. It also enhances how the company communicates and conveys its culture and philosophy. In addition, it clearly states the expectations. Disclosing compensation enables benchmarking across a particular industry or sector, helping you to keep in mind the factors that will ensure the company can remain competitive and attract and retain the right executive talent.

PART THREE
MAKING YOUR DREAMS COME TRUE

You now understand the DREAMS protocol, which is your blueprint to success, so let's move on to the practicalities.

SEVEN

Problems And Mistakes

There are various problems you might face in the process of pursuing a SPAC merger, and many mistakes you could make in implementation. This chapter runs through some of the most common of these.

Cashing in, not cashing out

Many company owners think that SPAC mergers are synonymous with "cashing out." But in reality, what you're doing is cashing in. The frame of mind behind cashing out is about trying to achieve as high a valuation as possible, which should not be the driving factor of a SPAC merger transaction. Instead, it should be about achieving a valuation that leaves a lot of room for the share price to grow. This is the reason why many de-SPAC mergers show poor price evolution and mediocre market performance: because the frame of mind of the parties going into the transaction is to try and achieve as high a valuation as possible, rather than the correct valuation.

To avoid this mistake, you should determine what a reasonable valuation is, apply a significant discount to that valuation, and then enter into the transaction. Keep in mind that when you're entering into a merger with a stock, you're not cashing out, you're:

- Cashing in

- Creating currency

- Making a way to create additional funding in the future

One of your objectives should be to leave investors and shareholders with a good taste in their mouths: a positive experience and memory of a transaction that's performed well in the aftermarket. Remember, when merging with a SPAC, all of the funds that are held in trust, as well as the new capital that you bring in, will go to fund the growth and operations of MergedCo. The capital is reinvested into the business and supports its ongoing expansion. The SPAC sponsors, along with you and your investors, become shareholders in a newly public company; all of your interests are aligned with the business's long-term success because all parties are issued with primary shares. No existing investors can cash out by selling secondary shares, which is what happens when you structure an IPO.

In an IPO, you have a sale of primary shares alongside the sale of secondary shares. Secondary shares are typically held by early investors, insiders, and founders, and the sale of secondary shares allows them to cash out early ahead of everyone else. Some think this is fair, given that these early investors initially supported the company and offered networks that provided expertise. The IPO allows them to monetize their stake and decide whether they want to reinvest in the business or invest in other start-ups. This is a key difference between an IPO and a SPAC: when you're doing a merger with the SPAC, you're not selling secondary shares of your business; you're fueling your business for growth going forward.

When you are public, life is different

A common issue is thinking everything will remain the same after going public. One of the big mistakes private company owners make when looking at going public is they focus only on the amount of funding they will receive. You must remember that post-merger you are managing a publicly listed company, which means you must do your duty and service to the public. The market rewards you for providing transparency and honesty and running a business according to the high standards that are imposed on publicly listed companies. In exchange, you get access to funding. Make no mistake, the company will need to be run according to higher standards of compliance and the highest standards of governance, so it is imperative to have a majority of non-executive and independent directors on your board. You will be subject to diversity criteria.

How you manage the company once it becomes public will be different from how you managed it when it was private. Failing to realize this is a mistake made by many entrepreneurs who go down the path of a merger with funding as their only aim and focus; once they receive the funding, they try to apply the same management techniques and operate with the same culture as before. They then find themselves frustrated by the fact that changes are being recommended or required by their board.

Investors need a face

Owners of private companies typically have to manage fewer shareholders, and another common mistake post-merger is failing to ensure consistent engagement with investors. You need a face to offer investors. This is something you can begin to work on pre-merger because, even if not listed, companies in many jurisdictions are considered public when they have fifty or more shareholders. Irrespective of whether you're publicly listed or not, it is crucial to maintain transparency and make an effort to maintain communication with shareholders and keep them in the loop.

One of the implications of being publicly listed is your continuous disclosure obligation (see Appendix 3). This necessitates that investors be made aware of any new information that could be material to their decision to sell or buy more shares. Taking too long to disclose that information may lead to situations where insiders trade with privileged information and you could face questions from the regulator. Confidential and strategic transaction discussions might also leak and affect the share price.

Any strategic agreements entered into by the company, or event LOIs for such contracts, must be announced using the 8-K form. Examples include a change in directors, the issuance of new shares or options to a new party, a merger discussion, etc. The longer you keep this information out of the public domain, the higher the chance it makes its way into the hands of a select few who could potentially take the opportunity to transact on the shares. This can lead to an insider trading investigation by the regulator. As such, it is important to have a dedicated person internally who will be the "face" of the company to investors and ensure that their queries and concerns are addressed promptly.

There are large and small shareholders, but the regulatory rules state that they all deserve the same access to information. No shareholder is too small to be worthy of consideration. For this reason, it is essential to have an efficient mechanism to communicate with all investors. Nowadays, plenty of service providers help handle this aspect of a company's management. Participating in conferences where you can give regular updates about the company's development is another good way of managing investor relations. In terms of who should handle the investor-facing function, it is crucial to have one ambassador, and sometimes the best ambassador is you. Could you transition to that role and let your team run the company?

Lack of a plan

I cannot say it often enough: right from the beginning, you must plan for this entire process. Once you are clear that you have a mandate to raise capital via a merger with a publicly listed vehicle, or you have made that decision, spending some time planning the entire operation is vital. This is what the DREAMS protocol, detailed in Chapter 5, is for.

In the first step of the protocol, you will plan for how you're going to organize the data and who will help you with that process, then research and reach out to the investors. This does not necessarily need to be time consuming, but good planning by ensuring you've got the right information package and the proper legal documents for an efficient outreach campaign is essential. Then, you need to identify established time windows when you can engage. Remember, as the founder and CEO of a private company raising funding, you will need to get on calls or video conferences with interested potential investors; they will want to hear from the horse's mouth what the business is about, and they will have questions. You must plan so that you can make yourself available for these calls. These counterparties are often situated in the US, but they can also be in Asia and Europe. Ensure you can block out time for these key meetings and that you're not flying around on holiday when your outreach campaign is happening. After that, planning for the rest of the activities in the protocol is all about finding an agreement between the parties and then mobilizing the resources. You may decide that the rest of the execution process can be delegated to your project manager or team.

It pays to plan. One of the major mistakes made by companies that want to raise funding is that they do not have a plan. What if the first agreement falls apart, and you need to go into a second agreement? Have you lined up your funding sources in case the timeline is not executed? You don't want to be running around with your hair on fire when you are halfway through the process. This means you need a Plan B and a Plan C in case, for example, the timeline gets longer, or there is an issue with the initial SPAC sponsor.

Don't run out of capital

Clients often come to us when they run out of capital and have no other options; they are in a desperate situation. This is why you should apply the DREAMS protocol early on, with particular focus on Steps 1 and 2: dataset, detail, documentation, and digital vault, and then risk management, research, and review of potential investors. At the same time, you have to have one eye on ensuring that you have enough capital to continue the day-to-day activities of the company. Nothing is worse than running out of capital while trying to raise more capital. It puts you in a weak position vis-a-vis the investors. You need to look ahead and prepare yourself so that when you are ready to proceed with the SPAC, you won't be forced down a particular path. You will also need to get alternative sources of capital in place in case the process takes longer than expected.

There are many reasons why companies run out of capital. One of the main ones is that they can be over-confident. They've got a bias toward optimism; they think their business is good, they are growing, and they don't need to think about securing additional capital now, they'll figure it out later. As a result, they are not planning proactively and rely on last-minute fundraising efforts. That is a major mistake.

At the same time, many founders don't necessarily have a deeper understanding of financial planning, cash flow management, and, more importantly, how capital markets work. They have received loans from traditional banks. When liquidity crises occur, as they do from time to time, they hope that the banks can save them, but banks are at the forefront of every liquidity crisis. As a result, companies that don't plan for the future sometimes run out of capital.

Another reason a company can run out of capital is because it's growing too quickly. Specific sectors, such as chip manufacturing, may require massive amounts of capital quickly. If a company is not careful about how it plans for its access to capital, it may suffer from a lack of liquidity.

Finally, one of the main reasons companies do not have access to capital when they need it is because they rely too much on cheap loans from banks. Often this is because the founders and owners are reluctant to give up equity. They think they want to continue owning all of the company. This is a strategic mistake and limits their ability to explore alternative means of funding. By the time they finally come around to the idea of giving up equity, it may be too late; they then face a liquidity crunch, and will not be able to access the capital they require. To avoid this, companies should be proactive in creating their financial projections, identifying the funding needs, and building and maintaining relationships with different funding and financiers. They must be open to and plan for investment using the DREAMS protocol to secure financing from qualified institutional investors who can react quickly.

Conclusion

I n this book, you have learned to present your business in a way that makes it irresistible for institutional investors. You also have a better understanding of the incredible potential that merging with a SPAC can offer your company. You have learned about the numerous benefits of starting your approach to investment by applying the DREAMS protocol and going to SPAC sponsors first. They represent the entry to the ecosystem in which you can access millions of dollars in equity capital by partnering with experienced institutional investors who can help guide your company to new heights. However, knowledge alone isn't enough; to capitalize on this opportunity, you need to take action—and there's no better time than now.

At the time of writing this book, more than one hundred SPACs were looking to deploy US$7.4 billion of cash in private businesses before the end of 2024, according to data made available to the public by the SEC.[17]

In putting yourself out there and positioning your company for growth and expansion, it is fine to carry on conversations with family offices, private equity funds, and other alternative investment funds, but remember that these investors, though of an institutional nature, do not necessarily have a timeline by which they must deploy their cash.

The situation is the opposite for SPAC sponsors. They need to deploy their money and invest before the expiry date of their vehicle; otherwise, they will suffer significant economic losses. SPACs are the archetype of motivated institutional investors with cash to deploy soon, both in equity and as minority shareholders.

As publicly listed entities, all the information about SPACs is publicly available on the website of the SEC. Many specialty research services also provide data about SPACs, their size, and expiry dates. The contact names and addresses are on the first page of their respective registration statements. Go there and compile a list of SPACs that have been issued and are still looking for a target. A SPAC-target matching service also helps private companies connect with relevant SPACs. Go to www.dreamsprotocol.com for more

information on how to position your business in front
of institutional investors.

What does your future look like?

Imagine what your company could achieve with a
significant influx of capital. You could accelerate your
growth plans, expand into new markets, and invest in
cutting-edge technologies that will keep you ahead of
the competition. You could also use your newly issued
shares as a powerful currency to acquire other companies, further expanding your reach and capabilities.

However, the benefits extend far beyond the initial capital injection. You will also gain the prestige
of being a publicly listed company on a US stock
exchange, which unlocks a world of possibilities. This
status can open doors to new strategic partnerships
and lucrative contracts, attract top talent, and cement
your position as a leader in your industry. Plus, the
enhanced corporate governance requirements and
greater transparency of being a public company will
instill a culture of excellence within your organization
and help you gain the trust and confidence of investors, customers, and other stakeholders. You become a
player on the global stage, a beacon in your industry.

You have to take the first step to benefit from the
insights contained in this book. That's why I urge you
to start putting the DREAMS protocol into practice

right away. Begin by preparing and positioning your business and identifying potential SPAC partners and other institutional investors that align with your company's vision and values.

You can measure your readiness to face institutional investors by taking the free test at www.dreamsprotocol.com. This will give you an instant assessment of your ability to obtain investments from qualified institutional investors seeking to put capital at work in private companies as minority shareholders.

I know the process may seem daunting initially, but remember you are not in this alone (see Appendix 4). By following the roadmap laid out in the DREAMS protocol, you can navigate the fundraising process with confidence and come out on the other side with a stronger, more valuable company.

Launching your future

Congratulations on making it to the end of this book. Learning about the DREAMS protocol should have helped you visualize a bright and powerful future for your business. By going straight to motivated institutional investors, you will not only accelerate the development of your company, but you will also leave all your competitors in the dust.

Remember, the millions of dollars you secure aren't a windfall—they're the fuel you'll use to dominate your market. Imagine accelerating research and development, scaling your operations overnight, or acquiring that game-changing competitor—these things are all within reach, thanks to the strategic partnership with a SPAC and its institutional investors.

The DREAMS protocol isn't just a theoretical framework—it's a roadmap to success that will guide your company toward its full potential. The time for deliberation is over. You've analyzed the landscape, weighed the options, and now you possess the knowledge to navigate the exciting world of SPACs and institutional investors, and you have the formula to present your case so that you successfully attract the financing your business requires to dominate in your sector.

In the words of Walt Disney: "The way to get started is to quit talking and begin doing."[18]

Don't let this momentum fade—the market waits for no one. Start implementing the principles of the DREAMS protocol to transform your company. The opportunity is there for the taking; all you need is the courage and determination to seize it. This is your moment. Embrace the transformative power of DREAMS and let it be the launchpad that catapults your company to the top of its game.

Take the first step today.

Appendix 1
History Of SPACs

D avid Nussbaum and David Miller are credited as the grandfathers of SPACs as a modern financial instrument. They invented the SPAC "to give private firms another way to access everyday investors."[19] The issues with SPACs started with scandals that continued well into the '90s. In 1989, a group of Washington-based state securities regulators drafted a report stating that penny stock traders were losing more than $2 billion a year due to widespread fraud in the market. The report was directed to Congress before a penny stock fraud hearing. At that time, the size of the penny stock market was $10 billion across 13,000 listings. There was one company, the Stuart-James Company, that was singled out as one of the largest promoters of US penny stocks, and which was a significant concern of regulators watching this space. Stuart-James had fifty-two offices in twenty-two states, from which it marketed penny stocks widely. The report's recommendations included a suggestion to completely ban "blank-check offerings," which represented 70% of the penny stock issues in 1988, as well as the payment of bounties to informers who assisted in denouncing fraud cases:

"In 1989, 13,000 penny stock companies were trading on the Pink Sheets (now renamed 'OTC Markets'), and over $10 billion had been raised, of which 70% was in blank-check companies."[20]

Congress did not go as far as banning blank-check companies. Instead, it passed the Penny Stock Reform Act of 1990 (PSRA), which resulted in the SEC enacting special regulations for these types of offerings, under Rule 419.[21] Rule 419 defines a penny stock company as any company not listed nationally, with a share price below $4, stockholder equity of less than $5 million, or a market capitalization value of less than $50 million. The approach turned out to be effective against penny stock scams, but it also killed the market for blank-check companies in terms of new issues.

By 1993, investment banker David Nussbaum and lawyer David Miller had devised an innovative solution to the challenges faced by private companies looking to access public investment: SPACs, or modern blank-check companies. In the SPAC structure, the initial share price had to be above $4 and the stockholder equity above $5 million. In addition, the IPO proceeds needed to remain in a trust account until a business combination was approved by the target company, and, more crucially, the SPAC needed to acquire a target within a specified period (eighteen months) or it would have to return the capital to the investors.

The aim was to create an alternative route for businesses seeking funding, bypassing the traditional methods that often proved complex and time consuming while remaining in compliance with the SEC's Rule 419. While Nussbaum and Miller initially encountered skepticism and resistance due to the fraudulent associations of SPACs' predecessors from the 1980s, they focused on redesigning the offerings in line with the new rules established by the regulator.

Yet penny stocks fraud still occurred with relative frequency throughout the 1990s. In 1997, for example, the SEC ordered the commencement of administrative proceedings against a then-prominent player in the blank-check companies scene, GKN Securities. The action concerned GKN's failure to supervise its salespeople properly and exercise proper control over its sales activities.[22]

Despite the presence of bad actors in this space, the inventors of SPACs continued to collaborate with regulators to implement crucial safeguards that would protect investors and enhance transparency in the process. The most critical measures included in the reform are the option for investors to retrieve their money before a merger (the so-called "redemption right") and the increased disclosure obligations.

It is fair to say that the tireless efforts of Nussbaum's investment bank, EarlyBird Capital Inc, and Miller's law firm, Graubard Miller, have been instrumental in driving the SPAC boom. Today, their pioneering work is acknowledged as a cornerstone of this ecosystem, which is constantly evolving as the SEC works to close the regulatory arbitrages between SPACs and regular IPOs. Themselves, they would go on to launch more than a dozen SPACs that successfully merged with targets, before the market hit a pause.

In his paper "Money for nothing, shares for free," Ross Greenspan defines the second-generation SPAC period as the years between 2003 and 2011. It was during that era that hedge funds became significant players in SPAC IPOs, "motivated by securities arbitrage opportunities between the constituent parts of the SPAC unit once split and traded separately from each other."[23]

The 2013 movie *The Wolf of Wall Street*, set in 1987, is based on true stories of the fraudulent activities of Stratton Oakmont and Jordan Belfort, which involved penny stock manipulation, among other financial crimes.[24] *Boiler Room* (2000) is another movie set during the same era and is a gritty portrayal of the high-pressure sales tactics used to lure investors into fraudulent deals, by a group of young, ambitious stockbrokers who become embroiled in a penny stock fraud scheme.[25]

For many years after they were created, SPACs remained a relatively unknown capital instrument, mainly confined to the biotech space, but that changed in 2020. Around the time of the COVID-19 pandemic, the tide began to turn; prominent figures from the worlds of finance, technology, and entertainment began to take notice and lend their names to SPAC deals. By 2021, SPACs had raised a staggering $75 billion, accounting for over 70% of all IPOs that year.

The pandemic brought significant uncertainty in the financial markets and caused various and wide-ranging disruption due to a global drop in consumption caused by the shutdowns across the globe. In spring 2020, oil prices went briefly into negative territory, equity prices saw huge swings, and traditional IPO activity came to a sharp halt, with travel restrictions making it impossible to conduct fundraising roadshows. At that time, the market evolved and SPACs gained popularity due to their unique advantages: the ability to provide forward-looking projections to investors (not permissible in conventional IPOs) and the immediate availability of cash in trust.

A significant shift occurred within the market, and several high-profile entities, including DraftKings Inc, Virgin Galactic, and MP Materials decided to leverage

SPACs to go public. The average deal size catapulted upwards, and SPACs became an alternative source of investment banking fees for bulge-bracket institutions that had previously refrained from operating in this market. Suddenly, Deutsche Bank, Goldman Sachs, Morgan Stanley, and Credit Suisse dominated the SPAC issuance league tables. The fever around SPACs peaked in 2021, when the average SPAC IPO size reached US$320 million, versus US$176 million for traditional IPOs (page 2 of the Wilmerhale IPO report 2022).[26] DraftKings was the poster child of that era.

DraftKings[27] is a fantasy sports company that announced a merger with Diamond Eagle Acquisition Corp, a SPAC that had $500 million in cash in trust at the time. The transaction also included a PIPE deal of around $300 million. In this deal, Credit Suisse and Goldman Sachs drove the reverse merger. DraftKings had looked at going public several times before but suffered a stalled IPO in 2015 due to inclement market conditions. Then, in 2017, it failed to merge with FanDuel Inc as the US Federal Trade Commission pressured the company to abandon the idea. After a ruling by the Supreme Court in favor of commercial sports betting in 2018, DraftKings saw a sharp increase in revenues from its now-validated business model. By 2020, the decision to go public via a SPAC was strongly supported by Jason Robins, the company's CEO, who stated at the time, "Had we chosen a traditional IPO structure, odds are we wouldn't be closing it right now."[28] At the time of the merger, the market was in a sustained eleven-year bull run and presidential elections were approaching, with uncertainty in public markets and projections of an economic contraction.

As of the date of editing this book, the number of SPACs active in the market totals 240 companies that are either actively seeking a merger or have announced a business combination. The total amount of money locked up in trust accounts is US$50 billion across both categories.

SPACs are a permanent staple of equity capital markets regarding new issuance mechanisms. Still, they remain controversial and continue to be the object of further regulation from the SEC. As they continue to thrive, their ground-breaking contributions will shape the future of public investment for years to come.

Appendix 2
Notorious SPAC Deals

The shortest de-SPAC to bankruptcy filing

The award for the shortest time between the de-SPAC merger and bankruptcy goes to Near Intelligence and KludeIn I Acquisition Corp. On 19 May 2022, Near Intelligence Holdings Inc (the target) announced that it had negotiated and signed a BCA with KludeIn I Acquisition Corp, a SPAC with $172 million of cash in trust at the time of its IPO, and which was trading on the Nasdaq under the ticker INKA.[29]

Near Intelligence was founded in 2021 and focused on managing one of the largest databases of information on people, places, and products, comprising nearly 1.6 billion unique user IDs in more than forty countries.

They essentially sold datasets containing information about the shopping, traveling, and dining habits of the consumers they had profiled. The buyers of these datasets were advertising and marketing companies.

KludeIn I Acquisition Corp went public in an IPO on 7 January 2021, and in May 2022, it announced the merger agreement with Near Intelligence.[30]

The notice of effectiveness for the merger was granted on 13 February 2023. On 8 December 2023, the company released an 8-K report stating that it had filed a voluntary petition for relief under Chapter 11 of the Bankruptcy Code. That equates to 298 days between effectiveness and Chapter 11.

The largest de-SPAC merger (and the largest PIPE)

The award for the largest ever de-SPAC merger to date goes to Grab (the target) and Altimeter Growth Corp (AGC: Nasdaq). The business combination, which closed on 1 December 2021, was done at a valuation close to $40 billion.

Grab is an application that provides mobility, food delivery, and financial services. It operates in eight Southeast Asian countries, covering 400 cities across Cambodia, Indonesia, Malaysia, Myanmar, the Philippines, Singapore, Thailand, and Vietnam. It is an Asia-based equivalent of Uber. The PIPE deal accompanying the transaction was equally significant, at $4 billion. It was arranged and led by Altimeter Capital, the sponsor of the SPAC.[31]

The largest SPAC IPO

The largest ever SPAC IPO to date was Pershing Square Tontine Holdings (PSTH: Nasdaq). The IPO date was 22 July 2020, and the deal, led by Citigroup, raised $4 billion. The share price used for the IPO was $20, instead of the customary $10. The sponsor behind the deal was Bill Ackman, a famous Wall Street dealmaker. At the time of issuance, this SPAC was the largest pool of cash equity designated for a single company as minority investment worldwide. Attached to the deal was a structured capital instrument of $1 billion in the form of a forward purchase agreement. The focus of investment was generic and not centered on any sector. The main challenge for the sponsor, and the real limiting factor of this deal, was that the size of any potential target had to be in the tens of billions of dollars. Pershing Square tried to recut the deal and bring in more than one company under its roof, but their attempts were thwarted by the SEC. Eventually, the SPAC had to liquidate and return all its capital in trust to the shareholders. The liquidation event was announced in July 2022.[32]

De-SPAC merger with an asset that belonged to an already listed company

In October 2022, European Lithium (EUR: ASX) announced that it had signed a BCA with Sizzle Acquisition Corp (SZZL), which involved selling one of its main assets, codenamed Wolfsberg. The Wolfsberg project is a lithium exploration asset located in Austria. The interesting detail about this deal is that European Lithium was a company already publicly listed on the Australian Securities Exchange (Ticker: EUR) and had a market capitalization of around US$70 million at the time. Under the terms of the BCA with Sizzle Acquisition Corp, it approved the sale of its main asset, the Wolfsberg project, at a valuation that was significantly higher than the valuation implied by its stock price, to the tune of US$750 million. The SEC approved the merger in February 2022, more than two years after the announcement of the merger agreement.[33]

Appendix 3
Learn To Read Public Disclosure Of SPACs

As a business owner, it is essential to learn where to find the information relevant to the SPAC you have identified as a candidate; it is also good to understand the necessary documentation the SPAC provides and know how to read and interpret some of its disclosures. This is not an extensive essay on the legalese associated with public corporation disclosures, but rather a summary of the most important statements.

Typically, publicly listed companies need to file a series of documents that are publicly accessible on the website of the SEC. Often, publicly listed companies also put a copy of these on their website.

Draft registration statement, or Form S-1

The first and most important document for you to consider when approaching a SPAC and its sponsors is Form S-1, the registration statement (F-1 in case of a non-US company seeking a listing on a US exchange). It is a relatively lengthy document, usually 100–150 pages, which contains all of the basic information about the SPAC and its executives, such as the chief executive officers and the lawyers. On the first page is a table that presents the amount of cash placed inside the trust, the number of shares and warrants, if there are warrants, and all of the essential information concerning the IPO. The document also contains the risk factors and other statements concerning the use of proceeds dividend policy, dilution capitalization, the track record of the management, and the identities of the principal shareholders. This document needs to exist when the SPAC does its IPO.

8-K

The next type of public disclosure you need to learn to recognize as a company owner looking to merge with a SPAC is 8-K statements. An 8-K statement is also known as a current report and is used to disclose "material information" to the public. Typically, whenever there is a significant event that could affect the share price of the SPAC or affect the view that shareholders have about the listed company, the company has four days to report that event to the stock exchange and to file an 8-K report. Examples of evidence that must be reported include a change of directors on the board, a significant corporate action, or an investigation into the company by the regulator. Another instance where an 8-K disclosure is necessary is if an LOI or a Memorandum of Understanding is signed between the SPAC and another party. To understand more about a SPAC and its sponsors, it is helpful to download and read the 8-K reports they have filed, where you can see the significant events that have impacted its history.

10-K

The 10-K report is the annual report required by the SEC. It provides a complete and comprehensive picture of the company's financial performance. Typically, a company must file a 10-K within two months of the end of the fiscal year. Knowing where to find and access that report, and contrast the information with the representations made by the management, is also helpful.

10-Q

The 10-Q is a quarterly report focused on the financials and operations over the last quarter. Think of the 10-Q as a subset of the 10-K reports. It's essentially the same type of report but covers a quarter instead of an entire year.

S-4

Form S-4 is filed by the SPAC whenever any material information related to a merger or acquisition occurs. Once the SEC gives the green light to the acquisition or the merger, the SPAC must file an S-4 as soon as possible to provide public notice of the transaction.

The S-4 indicates that the company has decided to enter into a significant transaction, such as a merger or acquisition. As the owner of a private company looking to potentially merge with a SPAC, you would want to see whether the SPAC had already filed for a merger in the past. If it had filed for one but hadn't closed, you may wish to inquire about the problem. Why couldn't they go ahead with the merger? Was there an issue concerning the target company, or was there an issue for the shareholders of the SPAC? The S-4 gives helpful information about the history and type of mergers and acquisitions-related actions the company has been involved in.

Appendix 4
Online Resources

- SPAC Insider (www.spacinsider.com)

- SPAC Research (www.spacresearch.com)

- SPAC Analytics (www.spacanalytics.com)

- SPAC Data (https://spacdata.com)

- SPAC Monitor (https://spacmonitor.com)

- SEC company filing information (www.sec.gov/search-filings)

- News on SPACs (www.egsllp.com/category/resources/spacs)

- SPAC Conference (https://news.spacconference.com)

- SPAC Track (www.listingtrack.io/redirection)

Notes

1 Private Securities Litigation Reform Act (1995), US Congress, www.congress.gov/bill/104th-congress/house-bill/1058, accessed August 2024

2 SPAC Research Weekly Newsletter (14 February 2022), www.spacresearch.com/newsletter?date=2022-02-14, accessed November 2024

3 C Barlow, M Chitwood, H Ellin, R Fox, M Gasaway, E Micheletti and G Noel, *De-SPAC Transition Trends in 2023* (LexisNexis/Practical Guidance, 2023), www.skadden.com/-/media/files/publications/2023/06/de_spac_transaction_trends_in_2023.pdf?rev=a0def9cfccae4a3fa2b31b3efc20e548#:~:text=In%202021%2C%2095%25%20of%20SPAC,of%20

the%20SPAC%20trust%20account, accessed
August 2024

4 The 7th Annual SPAC Conference 2024
livestream: https://spacconference.com,
accessed August 2024

5 Kroll, *Special Purpose Acquisition Companies: 2020
year end review* (Kroll, 2024), www.kroll.com/-/
media/kroll-images/pdfs/special-purpose-
acquisition-companies-2023-year-end-review-
and-2024-outlook.pdf, accessed August 2024

6 SPAC Analytics: www.spacanalytics.com,
accessed August 2024

7 SPAC Analytics: www.spacanalytics.com,
accessed August 2024

8 AJ Harris, "Waiting on Waitr: How a Louisiana
federal court decision may shape the oncoming
billion dollar wave of SPAC securities
litigation", Fordham Blog (2 April 2021), www.
fordhamiplj.org/2021/04/02/waiting-on-waitr-
how-a-louisiana-federal-court-decision-may-
shape-the-oncoming-billion-dollar-wave-of-
spac-securities-litigation/, accessed August 2024

9 Nasdaq Listing Center Rulebook search:
https://listingcenter.nasdaq.com/rulebook/
nasdaq/rules/Nasdaq%205600%20Series,
accessed August 2024

10 SPAC Analytics: www.spacanalytics.com/,
accessed August 2024

11 E Yiu, "Hong Kong listing reforms for SPACs,
pre-revenue tech companies, foiled by high
threshold, interest-rate cycle, experts say",

SCMP Plus (1 January 2024), www.scmp.com/
business/article/3246859/hong-kong-listing-
reforms-spacs-pre-revenue-tech-companies-
foiled-high-threshold-interest-rate-cycle

12 Statista, "Number of special purpose acquisition
company SPAC IPOs in Europe to 1st quarter
2022, by issuer country", Statista Research
Department (6 June 2024), www.statista.com/
statistics/1312137/number-spac-ipos-europe-
by-country, accessed August 2024

13 Nasdaq Listing Center Rulebook search:
https://listingcenter.nasdaq.com/rulebook/
nasdaq/rules/Nasdaq%205400%20Series,
accessed August 2024

14 PR Newswire, "NewGenIvf and A SPAC I
announce shareholder approval of business
combination", PR Newswire (5 March 2024),
www.prnewswire.com/news-releases/
newgenivf-and-a-spac-i-announce-shareholder-
approval-of-business-combination-302079817.
html, accessed August 2024; Jensyn, "Jensyn
Acquisition Corp. completes business
combination with Peck Electric", Global
Newswire (20 June 2019), www.globenewswire.
com/en/news-release/2019/06/20/1871922/0/
en/Jensyn-Acquisition-Corp-Completes-
Business-Combination-with-Peck-Electric.
html, accessed August 2024; VivoPower
International, "VivoPower announces
binding heads of agreement to merge Tembo
into NASDAQ listed CCTS at an indicative

US$838m equity value", Global Newswire (2 April 2024), www.globenewswire.com/news-release/2024/04/02/2856229/0/en/VivoPower-announces-binding-heads-of-agreement-to-merge-Tembo-into-NASDAQ-listed-CCTS-at-an-indicative-US-838m-Equity-Value.html, accessed August 2024
Jet AI,"Jet Token Inc. to become publicly listed via business combination with Oxbridge Acquisition Corp. and change name to Jet AI Inc.", Jet AI (27 February 2023), https://investors.jet.ai/news-releases/news-release-details/jet-token-inc-become-publicly-listed-business-combination, accessed August 2024

15 Note that Nasdaq requires a minimum market cap for companies to initially go public. Then, due to market changes, the market cap can drop.

16 Dorsey, "Thinking of listing on the NASDAQ?", Dorsey & Whitney LLP Publications (4 April 2024), www.dorsey.com/newsresources/publications/client-alerts/2024/4/listing-on-nasdaq#:~:text=A%20total%20of%203%2C584%20companies,those%20companies%20being%20international%20enterprises, accessed August 2024

17 See Spacresearch.com

18 Walt Disney interview with Hedda Hopper, *Lima News Ohio* (15 July 1957), www.newspapers.com/image/690959513

19 A Ramkumar, "SPAC pioneers reap the rewards after waiting nearly 30 years", *Wall Street Journal*

(9 March 2021), www.wsj.com/articles/they-created-the-spac-in-1993-now-theyre-reaping-the-rewards-11615285801, accessed August 2024

20 GA Robb, "Fraud cited in penny stocks", *New York Times* (7 September 1989), www.nytimes.com/1989/09/07/business/fraud-cited-in-penny-stocks.html, accessed August 2024

21 Securities Enforcement Remedies and Penny Stock Reform Act of 1990 (15 October 1990), US Congress, www.congress.gov/bill/101st-congress/senate-bill/647, accessed August 2024

22 JG Katz, Administrative proceedings, GKN Securities (Securities and Exchange Commission, 1997), www.sec.gov/files/litigation/admin/3438173.txt

23 R Greenspan, "Money for nothing, shares for free: A brief history of the SPAC" (2021), https://papers.ssrn.com/sol3/papers.cfm?abstract_id=3832710, accessed August 2024

24 M Scorsese, *The Wolf of Wall Street*, Paramount Pictures (2013)

25 B Younger, *Boiler Room*, New Line Cinema (2000)

26 Deloitte Insights, *The SPACS Boom: Europe picks up the pace* (Deloitte Insights, 2021), www2.deloitte.com/content/dam/insights/articles/154482-spacs-in-europe/DI_The-SPACs-boom.pdf, accessed August 2024; Wilmer Hale, *IPO Report 2022* (Wilmer Hale 2022) p2, www.wilmerhale.com/insights/publications/2022-ipo-report, accessed August 2024

27 Wikipedia, DraftKings: https://en.wikipedia.org/wiki/DraftKings

28 C Tse and E Novy-Williams, "DraftKings rises 10% in public debut during freeze on sports", Bloomberg UK (24 April 2020), www.bloomberg.com/news/articles/2020-04-24/draftkings-defies-odds-to-go-public-during-freeze-on-sports?embedded-checkout=true, accessed August 2024

29 N Nishant and M Saini, "Data intelligence firm Near to go public via $1 billion SPAC deal", Reuters (19 May 2022), www.reuters.com/markets/deals/data-intelligence-firm-near-go-public-via-1-billion-spac-deal-2022-05-19, accessed August 2024

30 KludeIn I Acquisition Corp. and Near Intelligence Holdings Inc., "Near appoints Jon Zorio as Chief Revenue Officer to drive next phase of Company growth; appoints Jay Angelo as General Counsel", Near press release (21 September 2022), www.sec.gov/Archives/edgar/data/1826671/000121390022057656/ea166122-425_kludein1acq.htm, accessed August 2024

31 Grab Press Centre, "Grab to trade on Nasdaq following successful business combination with Altimeter", Grab (2 December 2021), www.grab.com/sg/press/others/grab-to-trade-on-nasdaq-following-successful-business-combination-with-altimeter, accessed August 2024

32 Businesswire, "Pershing Square Tontine
Holdings, Ltd. will redeem its public
shares and will not consummate an initial
business combination", Businesswire (11
July 2022), www.businesswire.com/news/
home/20220711005904/en/Pershing-Square-
Tontine-Holdings-Ltd.-Will-Redeem-Its-Public-
Shares-and-Will-Not-Consummate-an-Initial-
Business-Combination, accessed 24 September
2024

33 Critical Metals Corp., "Critical Metals, Europe's
first fully licensed lithium mine agrees to
go public on the Nasdaq through a business
combination with Sizzle Acquisition Corp",
Critical Metals Corp. press release (27 October
2022), https://criticalmetalscorp.com/wp-
content/uploads/2022/11/Project-Element-
BCA-Release-10.27.22-Correction-Release-Final.
pdf, accessed August 2024

Acknowledgments

To my extraordinary team and colleagues, who have been the backbone of this journey. Your tireless dedication, unwavering support, and remarkable expertise have shaped the insights and experiences shared within these pages. I am forever grateful for your hard work, loyalty, and the countless hours we have spent together navigating the complex world of SPACs. Your passion and commitment to excellence have been a constant source of inspiration.

To my amazing wife; my rock, and my guiding light. Your love, patience, and unwavering belief in me are the foundation upon which I stand. Through the long nights, the endless meetings, and the challenges we have faced, you have been my steadfast supporter, confidante, and source of strength. Your sacrifices and understanding have made this book possible, and I am forever indebted to you for your love and partnership.

This book is a testament to the collective efforts, knowledge, and passion of everyone who has been a part of this remarkable journey. Your contributions, both large and small, have left an indelible mark on these pages and my life. Thank you for joining me on this adventure.

With deepest gratitude.

The Author

Daniel Mamadou-Blanco has spent more than two decades across Europe, the Middle East, Africa, and Asia Pacific and has established relationships with key stakeholders and decision-makers across the specialty metals sector. His network includes global up, mid, and downstream companies. Before this, Daniel was managing director at Deutsche Bank, Goldman Sachs, and Nomura, focusing on debt and equity capital markets.

🌐 www.dreamsprotocol.com

f www.facebook.com/danielmamadou

- [in] www.linkedin.com/in/danielmamadou
- [instagram] www.instagram.com/danmamadou
- [X] www.x.com/DPMBlanco

www.ingramcontent.com/pod-product-compliance
Lightning Source LLC
Chambersburg PA
CBHW071552200326
41519CB00021BB/6712